For Alexander
from Aunt Grace -

Elizabeth Newsome

May 17th 1920.

E.A.C.

Friendship

THE WORKS of HUGH BLACK

FRIENDSHIP

By HUGH BLACK

With an
Introductory Note by
W. ROBERTSON NICOLL, D.D.

Chicago • New York • Toronto
FLEMING H. REVELL COMPANY
London • Edinburgh

EQUIDEM, ex omnibus rebus, quas mihi aut Fortuna aut Natura tribuit, nihil habeo quod cum amicitia Scipionis possum comparare.

CICERO.

INTREAT me not to leave thee,
And to return from following after thee :
For whither thou goest, I will go ;
And where thou lodgest, I will lodge :
Thy people shall be my people,
And thy God my God :
Where thou diest, will I die,
And there will I be buried :
The Lord do so to me, and more also,
If aught but death part thee and me.

BOOK OF RUTH.

APPRECIATION

BY SIR WM. ROBERTSON NICOLL, D.D.

MR. HUGH BLACK'S wise and charming little book on Friendship is full of good things winningly expressed, and, though very simply written, is the result of real thought and experience. Mr. Black's is the art that conceals art. For young men, especially, this volume will be a golden possession, and it can hardly fail to affect their after lives. Mr. Black says well that the subject of friendship is less thought of among us now than it was in the old world. Marriage has come to mean infinitely more. Communion with God in Christ has become to multitudes the primal fact of life. Nevertheless the need for friendship remains. — "British Weekly."

FRIENDSHIP is to be valued for what there is in it, not for what can be gotten out of it. When two people appreciate each other because each has found the other convenient to have around, they are not friends, they are simply acquaintances with a business understanding. To seek friendship for its utility is as futile as to seek the end of a rainbow for its bag of gold. A true friend is always useful in the highest sense; but we should beware of thinking of our friends as brother members of a mutual-benefit association, with its periodical demands and threats of suspension for non-payment of dues.

TRUMBULL.

Contents

Contents

The Miracle of
Friendship

*B*UT, *far away from these, another sort*
    Of lovers linkëd in true heart's consent ;
Which lovëd not as these for like intent,
But on chaste virtue grounded their desire,
Far from all fraud or feignëd blandishment ;
Which, in their spirits kindling zealous fire,
Brave thoughts and noble deeds did evermore aspire.

Such were great Hercules and Hylas dear ;
True Jonathan and David trusty tried ;
Stout Theseus and Pirithöus his fere ;
Pylades and Orestes by his side ;
Mild Titus and Gesippus without pride ;
Damon and Pythias, whom death could not sever ;
All these, and all that ever had been tied
In bands of friendship, there did live forever ;
Whose lives although decay'd, yet loves decayëd never.

                SPENSER, *The Faerie Queene.*

The Miracle of Friendship

THE idea, so common in the ancient writers, is not all a poetic conceit, that the soul of a man is only a fragment of a larger whole, and goes out in search of other souls in which it will find its true completion. We walk among worlds unrealized, until we have learned the secret of love. We know this, and in our sincerest moments admit this, even though we are seeking to fill up our lives with other ambitions and other hopes.

It is more than a dream of youth that there may be here a satisfaction of the heart, without which, and in comparison with which, all worldly success is failure. In spite of the selfishness which seems to blight all life, our hearts tell us that there is possible a nobler relationship of disin-

15

terestedness and devotion. Friendship in
its accepted sense is not the highest of
the different grades in that relationship,
but it has its place in the kingdom of
love, and through it we bring ourselves
into training for a still larger love. The
natural man may be self-absorbed and
self-centred, but in a truer sense it is
natural for him to give up self and link
his life on to others. Hence the joy with
which he makes the great discovery, that
he is something to another and another
is everything to him. It is the higher-
natural for which he has hitherto existed.
It is a miracle, but it happens.

The cynic may speak of the now obsolete sentiment of friendship, and he can
find much to justify his cynicism. Indeed, on the first blush, if we look at the
relative place the subject holds in ancient
as compared with modern literature, we
might say that friendship is a sentiment
that is rapidly becoming obsolete. In
Pagan writers friendship takes a much

16

Friendship

larger place than it now receives. The
subject bulks largely in the works of
Plato, Aristotle, Epictetus, Cicero. And
among modern writers it gets most importance in the writings of the more
Pagan-spirited, such as Montaigne. In
all the ancient systems of philosophy,
friendship was treated as an integral part
of the system. To the Stoic it was a
blessed occasion for the display of nobility and the native virtues of the human
mind. To the Epicurean it was the most
refined of the pleasures which made life
worth living. In the Nicomachean Ethics,
Aristotle makes it the culminating point,
and out of ten books gives two to the
discussion of Friendship. He makes it
even the link of connection between his
treatise on Ethics and his companion
treatise on Politics. It is to him both the
perfection of the individual life, and the
bond that holds states together. Friendship is not only a beautiful and noble
thing for a man, but the realization of it

is also the ideal for the state; for if citizens be friends, then justice, which is the great concern of all organized societies, is more than secured. Friendship is thus made the flower of Ethics, and the root of Politics.

Plato also makes friendship the ideal of the state, where all have common interests and mutual confidence. And apart from its place of prominence in systems of thought, perhaps a finer list of beautiful sayings about friendship could be culled from ancient writers than from modern. Classical mythology also is full of instances of great friendship, which almost assumed the place of a religion itself.

It is not easy to explain why its part in Christian ethics is so small in comparison. The change is due to an enlarging of the thought and life of man. Modern ideals are wider and more impersonal, just as the modern conception of the state is wider. The Christian ideal of

Friendship

love even for enemies has swallowed up
the narrower ideal of philosophic friendship. Then possibly also the instinct
finds satisfaction elsewhere in the modern man. For example, marriage, in
more cases now than ever before, sup-
plies the need of friendship. Men and
women are nearer in intellectual pur-
suits and in common tastes than they
have ever been, and can be in a truer
sense companions. And the deepest explanation of all is that the heart of man
receives a religious satisfaction impossible before. Spiritual communion makes
a man less dependent on human intercourse. When the heaven is as brass
and makes no sign, men are thrown
back on themselves to eke out their
small stores of love.

At the same time friendship is not an
obsolete sentiment. It is as true now as
in Aristotle's time that no one would care
to live without friends, though he had all
other good things. It is still necessary to

19

John 15

"Ye are
friends"

our life in its largest sense. The danger
of sneering at friendship is that it may be
discarded or neglected, not in the interests
of a more spiritual affection, but to minister to a debased cynical self-indulgence.
There is possible to-day, as ever, a gener·
ous friendship which forgets self. The
history of the heart-life of man proves
this. What records we have of such in
the literature of every country! Peradven-
ture for a good man men have even dared
to die. Mankind has been glorified by
countless silent heroisms, by unselfish service, and sacrificing love. Christ, who
always took the highest ground in His
estimate of men, and never once put man's
capacity for the noble on a low level,
made the high-water mark of human
friendship the standard of His own great
action, "Greater love hath no man than
this, that a man lay down his life for his
friends." This high-water mark has often
been reached. Men have given themselves
to each other, with nothing to gain, with

John II.

Friendship

no self-interest to serve, and with no keeping back part of the price. It is false to
history to base life on selfishness, to leave
out of the list of human motives the highest of all. The miracle of friendship has
been too often enacted on this dull earth of
ours, to suffer us to doubt either its possibility or its wondrous beauty.

The classic instance of David and Jonathan represents the typical friendship.
They met, and at the meeting knew each
other to be nearer than kindred. By
subtle elective affinity they felt that they
belonged to each other. Out of all the
chaos of the time and the disorder of
their lives, there arose for these two souls
a new and beautiful world, where there
reigned peace, and love, and sweet content. It was the miracle of the death
of self. Jonathan forgot his pride, and
David his ambition. It was as the smile
of God which changed the world to them.
One of them it saved from the tempta-
tions of a squalid court, and the other

from the sourness of an exile's life.
Jonathan's princely soul had no room for
envy or jealousy. David's frank nature
rose to meet the magnanimity of his
friend.

In the kingdom of love there was no
disparity between the king's son and the
shepherd boy. Such a gift as each gave
and received is not to be bought or sold.
It was the fruit of the innate nobility of
both: it softened and tempered a very
trying time for both. Jonathan with-
stood his father's anger to shield his
friend: David was patient with Saul for
his son's sake. They agreed to be true
to each other in their difficult position.
Close and tender must have been the
bond, which had such fruit in princely
generosity and mutual loyalty of soul.
Fitting was the beautiful lament, when
David's heart was bereaved at tragic
Gilboa, "I am distressed for thee, my
brother Jonathan: very pleasant hast
thou been unto me: thy love to me was

Friendship

wonderful, passing the love of women."
Love is always wonderful, a new creation,
fair and fresh to every loving soul. It is
the miracle of spring to the cold dull earth.

When Montaigne wrote his essay on
Friendship, he could do little but tell
the story of his friend. The essay con-
tinually reverts to this, with joy that he
had been privileged to have such a friend,
with sorrow at his loss. It is a chapter
of his heart. There was an element of
necessity about it, as there is about all
the great things of life. He could not
account for it. It came to him without
effort or choice. It was a miracle, but it
happened. "If a man should importune
me to give a reason why I loved him, I
can only answer, because it was he, because it was I." It was as some secret
appointment of heaven. They were both
grown men when they first met, and death
separated them soon. "If I should com-
pare all my life with the four years I had
the happiness to enjoy the sweet society

of this excellent man, it is nothing but
smoke ; an obscure and tedious night from
the day that I lost him. I have led a sorrowful and languishing life ever since. I
was so accustomed to be always his second
in all places and in all interests, that me-
thinks I am now no more than half a
man, and have but half a being." We
would hardly expect such passion of love
and regret from the easy-going, genial,
garrulous essayist.

The joy that comes from a true communion of heart with another is perhaps
one of the purest and greatest in the
world, but its function is not exhausted
by merely giving pleasure. Though we
may not be conscious of it, there is a
deeper purpose in it, an education in the
highest arts of living. We may be en-
ticed by the pleasure it affords, but its
greatest good is got by the way. Even
intellectually it means the opening of a
door into the mystery of life. Only love
understands after all. It gives insight.

24

Friendship

We cannot truly know anything without
sympathy, without getting out of self and
entering into others. A man cannot be
a true naturalist, and observe the ways of
birds and insects accurately, unless he can
watch long and lovingly. We can never
know children, unless we love them. Many
of the chambers of the house of life are
forever locked to us, until love gives us
the key.

To learn to love all kinds of nobleness
gives insight into the true significance of
things, and gives a standard to settle
their relative importance. An uninter-
ested spectator sees nothing, or, what is
worse, sees wrongly. Most of our mean
estimates of human nature in modern literature, and our false realisms in art, and
our stupid pessimisms in philosophy, are
due to an unintelligent reading of surface
facts. Men set out to note and collate
impressions, and make perhaps a scien-
tific study of slumdom, without genuine
interest in the lives they see, and there-

fore without true insight into them. They miss the inwardness, which love alone can supply. If we look without love we can only see the outside, the mere form and expression of the subject studied. Only with tender compassion and loving sympathy can we see the beauty even in the eye dull with weeping and in the fixed face pale with care. We will often see noble patience shining through them, and loyalty to duty, and virtues and graces unsuspected by others.

The divine meaning of a true friendship is that it is often the first unveiling of the secret of love. It is not an end in itself, but has most of its worth in what it leads to, the priceless gift of seeing with the heart rather than with the eyes. To love one soul for its beauty and grace and truth is to open the way to appreciate all beautiful and true and gracious souls, and to recognize spiritual beauty wherever it is seen.

The possibility at least of friendship

Friendship

must be a faith with us. The cynical attitude is an offence. It is possible to find in the world true-hearted, leal, and faithful dealing between man and man. To doubt this is to doubt the divine in life. Faith in man is essential to faith in God. In spite of all deceptions and dis-illusionments, in spite of all the sham fellowships, in spite of the flagrant cases of self-interest and callous cruelty, we must keep clear and bright our faith in the possibilities of our nature. The man who hardens his heart because he has been imposed on has no real belief in virtue, and with suitable circumstances could become the deceiver instead of the deceived. The great miracle of friend-ship with its infinite wonder and beauty may be denied to us, and yet we may believe in it. To believe that it is possi-ble is enough, even though in its superb-est form it has never come to us. To possess it, is to have one of the world's sweetest gifts.

The Miracle of

Aristotle defines friendship as one soul abiding in two bodies. There is no explaining such a relationship, but there is no denying it. It has not deserted the world since Aristotle's time. Some of our modern poets have sung of it with as brave a faith as ever poet of old. What splendid monuments to friendship we possess in Milton's *Lycidas* and Tennyson's *In Memoriam!* In both there is the recognition of the spiritual power of it, as well as the joy and comfort it brought. The grief is tempered by an awed wonder and a glad memory.

The finest feature of Rudyard Kipling's work and it is a constant feature of it, is the comradeship between commonplace soldiers of no high moral or spiritual attainment, and yet it is the strongest force in their lives, and on occasion makes heroes of them. We feel that their faithfulness to each other is almost the only point at which their souls are reached. The threefold cord of his soldiers, vulgar

Friendship

in mind and common in thought as they
are, is a cord which we feel is not easily
broken, and it is their friendship and loyalty to each other which save them from
utter vulgarity.

In Walt Whitman there is the same insight into the force of friendship in ordinary life, with added wonder at the
miracle of it. He is the poet of comrades, and sings the song of companionship more than any other theme. He
ever comes back to the lifelong love of
comrades. The mystery and the beauty
of it impressed him.

O tan-faced prairie-boy,
Before you came to camp came many a welcome
    gift,
Praises and presents came and nourishing food,
    till at last among the recruits
You came, taciturn, with nothing to give — we
    but looked on each other,
When lo! more than all the gifts of the world you
    gave me.

After all, in spite of the vulgar material-
ism of our day, we do feel that the spirit-

ual side of life is the most important,
and brings the only true joy. And friendship in its essence is spiritual. It is the
free, spontaneous outflow of the heart,
and is a gift from the great Giver.

Friends are born, not made. At least
it is so with the higher sort. The marriage of souls is a heavenly mystery, which
we cannot explain, and which we need
not try to explain. The method by
which it is brought about differs very
much, and depends largely on temperament. Some friendships grow, and
ripen slowly and steadily with the years.
We cannot tell where they began, or
how. They have become part of our
lives, and we just accept them with
sweet content and glad confidence. We
have discovered that somehow we are
rested, and inspired, by a certain companionship; that we understand and are
understood easily.

Or it may come like love at first sight,
by the thrill of elective affinity. This

latter is the more uncertain, and needs to
be tested and corrected by the trial of the
years that follow. It has to be found
out whether it is really spiritual kinship,
or mere emotional impulse. It is a matter of temper and character. A naturally
reserved person finds it hard to open his
heart, even when his instinct prompts
him ; while a sociable, responsive nature
is easily companionable. It is not always
this quick attachment, however, which
wears best, and that is the reason why
youthful friendships have the character
of being so fickle. They are due to a
natural instinctive delight in society.
Most young people find it easy to be
agreeable, and are ready to place themselves under new influences.

But whatever be the method by which
a true friendship is formed, whether the
growth of time or the birth of sudden
sympathy, there seems, on looking back,
to have been an element of necessity. It
is a sort of predestined spiritual relation-

ship. We speak of a man meeting his fate, and we speak truly. When we look back we see it to be like destiny; life converged to life, and there was no getting out of it even if we wished it. It is not that we made a choice, but that the choice made us. If it has come gradually, we waken to the presence of the force which has been in our lives, and has come into them never hasting but never resting, till now we know it to be an eternal possession. Or, as we are going about other business, never dreaming of the thing which occurs, the unexpected happens; on the road a light shines on us, and life is never the same again.

In one of its aspects, faith is the recognition of the inevitableness of providence; and when it is understood and accepted, it brings a great consoling power into the life. We feel that we are in the hands of a Love that orders our ways, and the knowledge means serenity and peace.

Friendship

The fatality of friendship is gratefully accepted, as the fatality of birth. To the faith which sees love in all creation, all life becomes harmony, and all sorts of loving relationships among men seem to be part of the natural order of the world. Indeed, such miracles are only to be looked for, and if absent from the life of man would make it hard to believe in the love of God.

The world thinks we idealize our friend, and tells us that love is proverbially blind. Not so : it is only love that sees, and thus can " win the secret of a weed's plain heart." We only see what dull eyes never see at all. If we wonder what another man sees in his friend, it should be the wonder of humility, not the supercilious wonder of pride. He sees something which we are not permitted to witness. Beneath and amongst what looks only like worthless slag, there may glitter the pure gold of a fair character. That anybody in the

3   33

world should be got to love us, and to
see in us not what colder eyes see, not
even what we are but what we may be,
should of itself make us humble and
gentle in our criticism of others' friendships. Our friends see the best in us,
and by that very fact call forth the best
from us.

The great difficulty in this whole subject is that the relationship of friendship should so often be one-sided. It
seems strange that there should be so
much unrequited affection in the world.
It seems almost impossible to get a completely balanced union. One gives so
much more, and has to be content to get
so much less. One of the most humili-
ating things in life is when another seems
to offer his friendship lavishly, and we
are unable to respond. So much love
seems to go a-begging. So few attachments seem complete. So much affection seems unrequited.

But are we sure it is unrequited? The

Friendship

difficulty is caused by our common selfish standards. Most people, if they had
their choice, would prefer to be loved
rather than to love, if only one of the
alternatives were permitted. That springs
from the root of selfishness in human
nature, which makes us think that possession brings happiness. But the glory
of life is to love, not to be loved; to give,
not to get; to serve, not to be served. It
may not be our fault that we cannot respond to the offer of friendship or love,
but it is our misfortune. The secret is
revealed to the other, and hid from us.
The gain is to the other, and the loss
is to us. The miracle is the love, and to
the lover comes the wonder of it, and the
joy.

The Culture of
Friendship

HOW were Friendship possible? In mutual de-votedness to the Good and True: otherwise impossible, except as Armed Neutrality, or hollow Commercial League. A man, be the Heavens ever praised, is sufficient for himself; yet were ten men, united in Love, capable of being and of doing what ten thousand singly would fail in. Infinite is the help man can yield to man.

CARLYLE, *Sartor Resartus.*

The Culture of Friendship

THE Book of Proverbs might almost be called a treatise on Friendship, so full is it of advice about the sort of person a young man should consort with, and the sort of person he should avoid. It is full of shrewd, and prudent, and wise, sometimes almost worldly-wise, counsel. It is caustic in its satire about false friends, and about the way in which friendships are broken. "The rich hath many friends," with an easily understood implication concerning their quality. "Every man is a friend to him that giveth gifts," is its sarcastic comment on the ordinary motives of mean men. Its picture of the plausible, fickle, lip-praising, and time-serving man, who blesseth his friend with a loud voice rising early in the morning, is a delicate piece of satire. The fragile connections among men, as easily broken as mended pottery, get illustration in the mischief-maker who loves to divide men. " A whisperer separateth chief friends." There is keen irony here over the quality of ordinary friendship, as well as condemnation of the tale-bearer and his sordid soul.

This cynical attitude is so common that we hardly expect such a shrewd book to speak heartily of the possibilities of human friendship. Its object rather is to put youth on its guard against the dangers and pitfalls of social life. It gives sound commercial advice about avoiding becoming surety for a friend. It warns against the tricks, and cheats, and bad faith, which swarmed in the streets of a city then, as they do still. It laughs, a little bitterly, at the thought that friendship can be as common as the eager, generous heart of youth imagines. It almost sneers at the gullibility of men

Friendship

in this whole matter. " He that maketh many friends doeth it to his own destruction."

And yet there is no book, even in classical literature, which so exalts the idea of friendship, and is so anxious to have it truly valued, and carefully kept. The worldly-wise warnings are after all in the interests of true friendship. To condemn hypocrisy is not, as is so often imagined, to condemn religion. To spurn the spurious is not to reject the true. A sneer at folly may be only a covert argument for wisdom. Satire is negative truth. The unfortunate thing is that most men, who begin with the prudential worldly-wise philosophy, end there. They never get past the sneer. Not so this wise book. In spite of its insight into the weakness of man, in spite of its frank denunciation of the common masquerade of friendship, it speaks of the true kind in words of beauty that have never been surpassed in all the many ap-

praisements of this subject. " A friend
loveth at all times, and is a brother born
for adversity. Faithful are the wounds
of a friend. Ointment and perfume rejoice the heart, so doth the sweetness of
a man's friend by hearty counsel. Thine
own friend and thy father's friend forsake not." These are not the words of
a cynic, who has lost faith in man.

True, this golden friendship is not a
common thing to be picked up in the
street. It would not be worth much if
it were. Like wisdom it must be sought
for as for hid treasures, and to keep it
demands care and thought. To think
that every goose is a swan, that every
new comrade is the man of your own
heart, is to have a very shallow heart.
Every casual acquaintance is not a hero.
There are pearls of the heart, which cannot be thrown to swine. Till we learn
what a sacred thing a true friendship is,
it is futile to speak of the culture of
friendship. The man who wears his

heart on his sleeve cannot wonder if daws peck at it. There ought to be a sanctuary, to which few receive admittance. It is great innocence, or great folly, and in this connection the terms are almost synonymous, to open our arms to everybody to whom we are introduced. The Book of Proverbs, as a manual on friendship, gives as shrewd and caustic warnings as are needed, but it does not go to the other extreme, and say that all men are liars, that there are no truth and faithfulness to be found. To say so is to speak in haste. There *is* a friend that sticketh closer than a brother, says this wisest of books. There is possible such a blessed relationship, a state of love and trust and generous comradehood, where a man feels safe to be himself, because he knows that he will not easily be misunderstood.

The word friendship has been abased by applying it to low and unworthy uses, and so there is plenty of copy still to be

got from life by the cynic and the satirist.
The sacred name of friend has been ban-
died about till it runs the risk of losing
its true meaning. Rossetti's versicle finds
its point in life —

" Was it a friend or foe that spread these lies? "
" Nay, who but infants question in such wise?
'T was one of my most intimate enemies. "

It is useless to speak of cultivating the
great gift of friendship unless we make
clear to ourselves what we mean by a
friend. We make connections and acquaintances, and call them friends. We
have few friendships, because we are not
willing to pay the price of friendship.

If we think it is not worth the price,
that is another matter, and is quite an in-
telligible position, but we must not use
the word in different senses, and then
rail at fate because there is no miracle of
beauty and joy about our sort of friendship. Like all other spiritual blessings it
comes to all of us at some time or other,

Friendship

and like them is often let slip. We have
the opportunities, but we do not make
use of them. Most men make friends
easily enough : few keep them. They do
not give the subject the care, and
thought, and trouble, it requires and deserves. We want the pleasure of society,
without the duty. We would like to get
the good of our friends, without burden-
ing ourselves with any responsibility
about keeping them friends. The commonest mistake we make is that we
spread our intercourse over a mass, and
have no depth of heart left. We lament
that we have no stanch and faithful
friend, when we have really not expended
the love which produces such. We want
to reap where we have not sown, the
fatuousness of which we should see as
soon as it is mentioned. "She that asks
her dear five hundred friends" (as Cow-
per satirically describes a well-known
type) cannot expect the exclusive affection, which she has not given.

The secret of friendship is just the secret of all spiritual blessing. The way to get is to give. The selfish in the end can never get anything but selfishness. The hard find hardness everywhere. As you mete, it is meted out to you.

Some men have a genius for friendship. That is because they are open and responsive, and unselfish. They truly make the most of life; for apart from their special joys, even intellect is sharpened by the development of the affections. No material success in life is comparable to success in friendship. We really do ourselves harm by our selfish standards. There is an old Latin proverb, [1] expressing the worldly view, which says that it is not possible for a man to *l*ove and at the same time to be wise. This is only true when wisdom is made equal to prudence and selfishness, and when love is made the same. Rather it is never given to a man to be wise in the

[1] *Non simul cuiquam conceditur, amare et sapere.*

Friendship

true and noble sense, until he is carried
out of himself in the purifying passion of
love, or the generosity of friendship.
The self-centred being cannot keep
friends, even when he makes them ; his
selfish sensitiveness is always in the
way, like a diseased nerve ready to be
irritated.

The culture of friendship is a duty, as
every gift represents a responsibility. It
is also a necessity; for without watchful
care it can no more remain with us than
can any other gift. Without culture it
is at best only a potentiality. We may
let it slip, or we can use it to bless our
lives. The miracle of friendship, which
came at first with its infinite wonder and
beauty, wears off, and the glory fades
into the light of common day. The early
charm passes, and the soul forgets the
first exaltation. We are always in danger of mistaking the common for the
commonplace. We must not look upon
it merely as the great luxury of life, or it

47

will cease to be even that. It begins
with emotion, but if it is to remain it
must become a habit. Habit is fixed
when an accustomed thing is organized
into life; and, whatever be the genesis
of friendship, it must become a habit, or
it is in danger of passing away as other
impressions have done before.

Friendship needs delicate handling.
We can ruin it by stupid blundering at the
very birth, and we can kill it by neglect.
It is not every flower that has vitality
enough to grow in stony ground. Lack
of reticence, which is only the outward
sign of lack of reverence, is responsible
for the death of many a fair friendship.
Worse still, it is often blighted at the
very beginning by the insatiable desire for piquancy in talk, which can forget the sacredness of confidence. " An
acquaintance grilled, scored, devilled, and
served with mustard and cayenne pepper,
excites the appetite; whereas a slice of
cold friend with currant jelly is but a

Friendship

sickly, unrelishing meat."[1] Nothing is given to the man who is not worthy to possess it, and the shallow heart can never know the joy of a friendship, for the keeping of which he is not able to fulfil the essential conditions. Here also it is true that from the man that hath not, is taken away even that which he hath.

The method for the culture of friendship finds its best and briefest summary in the Golden Rule. To do to, and for, your friend what you would have him do to, and for, you, is a simple compendium of the whole duty of friendship. The very first principle of friendship is that it is a mutual thing, as among spiritual equals, and therefore it claims reciprocity, mutual confidence and faithfulness. There must be sympathy to keep in touch with each other, but sympathy needs to be constantly exercised. It is a channel of communication, which has to be kept open, or it will soon be clogged and closed.

[1] Thackeray, *Roundabout Papers.*

The practice of sympathy may mean the cultivation of similar tastes, though that will almost naturally follow from the fellowship. But to cultivate similar tastes does not imply either absorption of one of the partners, or the identity of both. Rather, part of the charm of the intercourse lies in the difference, which exists in the midst of agreement. What is essential is that there should be a real desire and a genuine effort to understand each other. It is well worth while taking pains to preserve a relationship so full of blessing to both.

Here, as in all connections among men, there is also ample scope for patience. When we think of our own need for the constant exercise of this virtue, we will admit its necessity for others. After the first flush of communion has passed, we must see in a friend things which detract from his worth, and perhaps things which irritate us. This is only to say that no man is perfect. With tact, and tender-

50

ness and patience, it may be given us to help to remove what may be flaws in a fine character, and in any case it is foolish to forget the great virtues of our friend in fretful irritation at a few blemishes. We can keep the first ideal in our memory, even if we know that it is not yet an actual fact. We must not let our intercourse be coarsened, but must keep it sweet and delicate, that it may remain a refuge from the coarse world, a sanctuary where we leave criticism outside, and can breathe freely.

Trust is the first requisite for making a friend. How can we be anything but alone, if our attitude to men is one of armed neutrality, if we are suspicious, and assertive, and querulous, and over-cautious in our advances? Suspicion kills friendship. There must be some magnanimity and openness of mind, before a friendship can be formed. We must be willing to give ourselves freely and unreservedly.

The Culture of

Some find it easier than others to make advances, because they are naturally more trustful. A beginning has to be made somehow, and if we are moved to enter into personal association with another, we must not be too cautious in displaying our feeling. If we stand off in cold reserve, the ice, which trembled to thawing, is gripped again by the black hand of frost. There may be a golden moment which has been lost through a foolish reserve. We are so afraid of giving ourselves away cheaply — and it is a proper enough feeling, the value of which we learn through sad experience — but on the whole perhaps the warm nature, which acts on impulse, is of a higher type, than the over-cautious nature, ever on the watch lest it commit itself. We can do nothing with each other, we cannot even do business with each other, without a certain amount of trust. Much more necessary is it in the beginning of a deeper intercourse.

Friendship

And if trust is the first requisite for making a friend, *faithfulness* is the first requisite for keeping him. The way to have a friend is to be a friend. Faithfulness is the fruit of trust. We must be ready to lay hold of every opportunity which occurs of serving our friend. Life is made up to most of us of little things, and many a friendship withers through sheer neglect. Hearts are alienated, because each is waiting for some great occasion for displaying affection. The great spiritual value of friendship lies in the opportunities it affords for service, and if these are neglected it is only to be expected that the gift should be taken from us. Friendship, which begins with sentiment, will not live and thrive on sentiment. There must be loyalty, which finds expression in service. It is not the greatness of the help, or the intrinsic value of the gift, which gives it its worth, but the evidence it is of love and thoughtfulness.

53

Attention to detail is the secret of success in every sphere of life, and little kindnesses, little acts of considerateness, little appreciations, little confidences, are all that most of us are called on to perform, but they are all that are needed to keep a friendship sweet. Such thoughtfulness keeps our sentiment in evidence to both parties. If we never show our kind feeling, what guarantee has our friend, or even ourself, that it exists? Faithfulness in deed is the outward result of constancy of soul, which is the rarest, and the greatest, of virtues. If there has come to us the miracle of friendship, if there is a soul to which our soul has been drawn, it is surely worth while being loyal and true. Through the little occasions for helpfulness, we are training for the great trial, if it should ever come, when the fabric of friendship will be tested to the very foundation. The culture of friendship, and its abiding worth, never found nobler expression than in the beautiful

Friendship

proverb,[1] "A friend loveth at all times, and is a brother born for adversity."

Most men do not deserve such a gift from heaven. They look upon it as a convenience, and accept the privilege of love without the responsibility of it. They even use their friends for their own selfish purposes, and so never have true friends. Some men shed friends at every step they rise in the social scale. It is mean and contemptible to merely use men, so long as they further one's personal interests. But there is a nemesis on such heartlessness. To such can never come the ecstasy and comfort of mutual trust. This worldly policy can never truly succeed. It stands to reason that they cannot have brothers born for adversity, and cannot count on the joy of the love that loveth at all times; for they do not possess the quality which secures it. To act on the worldly policy, to treat a friend as if he might become an enemy,

[1] Proverbs xvii. 17, R. V. margin.

is of course to be friendless. To sacrifice a tried and trusted friend for any personal advantage of gain or position, is to deprive our own heart of the capacity for friendship.

The passion for novelty will sometimes lead a man to act like this. Some shallow minds are ever afflicted by a craving for new experiences. They sit very loosely to the past. They are the easy victims of the untried, and yearn perpetually for novel sensations. In this matter of friendship they are ready to forsake the old for the new. They are always finding a swan in every goose they meet. They have their reward in a widowed heart. Says Shakespeare in his great manner, —

> The friends thou hast and their adoption tried
> Grapple them to thy soul with hoops of steel,
> But do not dull thy palm with entertainment
> Of each new-hatched, unfledged comrade.

The culture of friendship must pass into the consecration of friendship, if it

56

Friendship

is to reach its goal. It is a natural evolution. Friendship cannot be permanent unless it becomes spiritual. There must be fellowship in the deepest things of the soul, community in the highest thoughts, sympathy with the best endeavors. We are bartering the priceless boon, if we are looking on friendship merely as a luxury, and not as a spiritual opportunity. It is, or can be, an occasion for growing in grace, for learning love, for training the heart to patience and faith, for knowing the joy of humble service. We are throwing away our chance, if we are not striving to be an inspiring and healthful environment to our friend. We are called to be our best to our friend, that he may be his best to us, bringing out what is highest and deepest in the nature of both.

The culture of friendship is one of the approved instruments of culture of the heart, without which a man has not truly

come into his kingdom. It is often only
the beginning, but through tender and
careful culture it may be an education
for the larger life of love. It broadens
out in ever-widening circles, from the
particular to the general, and from the
general to the universal — from the individual to the social, and from the social
to God. The test of religion is ultimately a very simple one. If we do not
love those whom we have seen, we cannot love those whom we have not seen.
All our sentiment about people at a
distance, and our heart-stirrings for the
distressed and oppressed, and our prayers
for the heathen, are pointless and fraudu-
lent, if we are neglecting the occasions
for service lying to our hand. If we do
not love our brethren here, how can we
love our brethren elsewhere, except as a
pious sentimentality? And if we do not
love those we have seen, how can we love
God whom we have not seen?

This is the highest function of friend-

Friendship

ship, and is the reason why it needs thoughtful culture. We should be led to God by the joy of our lives as well as by the sorrow, by the light as well as by the darkness, by human intercourse as well as by human loneliness. He is the Giver of every good gift. We wound His heart of love, when we sin against love. The more we know of Christ's spirit, and the more we think of the meaning of God's fathomless grace, the more will we be convinced that the way to please the Father and to follow the Son is to cultivate the graces of kindliness and gentleness and tenderness, to give ourselves to the culture of the heart. Not in the ecclesiastical arena, not in polemic for a creed, not in self-assertion and disputings, do we please our Master best, but in the simple service of love. To seek the good of men is to seek the glory of God. They are not two things, but one and the same. To be a strong hand in the dark to another in the time

Friendship

of need, to be a cup of strength to a
human soul in a crisis of weakness, is to
know the glory of life. To be a true
friend, saving his faith in man, and making him believe in the existence of love,
is to save his faith in God. And such
service is possible for all. We need not
wait for the great occasion and for the
exceptional opportunity. We can never
be without our chance, if we are ready to
keep the miracle of love green in our
hearts by humble service.

The primal duties shine aloft like stars.
The charities that soothe and heal and bless,
Are scattered at the feet of man like flowers.

The Fruits of
Friendship

TWO are better than one; because they have a good reward for their labor. For if they fall, the one will lift up his fellow: but woe to him that is alone when he falleth; for he hath not another to help him up. And if one prevail against him, two shall withstand him; and a threefold cord is not quickly broken. — ECCLESIASTES.

> O friend, my bosom said,
> Through thee alone the sky is arched,
> Through thee the rose is red,
> All things through thee take nobler form
> And look beyond the earth,
> And is the mill-round of our fate,
> A sun-path in thy worth.
> Me too thy nobleness has taught
> To master my despair;
> The fountains of my hidden life
> Are through thy friendship fair.
>
> EMERSON.

The
Fruits of
Friendship

IN our utilitarian age things are judged
by their practical value. Men ask of
everything, What is its use? Nothing is held to be outside criticism, neither
the law because of its authority, nor religion because of its sacredness. Every relationship in life also has been questioned,
and is asked to show the reason of its
existence. Even some relationships like
marriage, for long held to be above
question, are put into the crucible.

On the whole it is a good spirit, though
it can be abused and carried to an absurd
extreme. Criticism is inevitable, and
ought to be welcomed, provided we are
careful about the true standard to apply.
When we judge a thing by its use, we
must not have a narrow view of what
utility is. Usefulness to man is not con-

fined to mere material values. The common standards of the market-place cannot be applied to the whole of life. The things which cannot be bought cannot be sold, and the keenest valuator would be puzzled to put a price on some of these unmarketable wares.

When we seek to show what are the fruits of friendship, we may be said to put ourselves in line with the critical spirit of our age. But even if it were proven that a man could make more of his life materially by himself, if he gave no hostages to fortune, it would not follow that it is well to disentangle oneself from the common human bonds; for our *caveat* would here apply, that utility is larger than mere material gain.

But even from this point of view friendship justifies itself. Two are better than one; for they have a good reward for their labor. The principle of association in business is now accepted universally. It is found even to pay, to share work and

Friendship

profit. Most of the world's business is done by companies, or partnerships, or associated endeavor of some kind. And the closer the intimacy between the men so engaged, the intimacy of common desires and common purposes, and mutual respect and confidence, and, if possible, friendship, the better chance there is for success. Two are better than one from the point of view even of the reward of each, and a threefold cord is not quickly broken, when a single strand would snap.

When men first learned, even in its most rudimentary sense, that union is strength, the dawn of civilization began. For offence and for defence, the principle of association early proved itself the fittest for survival. The future is always with Isaac, not with Ishmael — with Jacob, not with Esau. In everything this is seen, in the struggle of races, or trade, or ideas. Even as a religious method to make an impact on the world, it is true. John of the Desert touched here a life, and there a life ; Jesus of Nazareth, seeking disciples, founding a society, moved the world to its heart.

It is not necessary to labor this point, that two are better than one, to a commercial age like ours, which, whatever it does not know, at least knows its arithmetic. We would say that it is self-evident, that by the law of addition it is double, and by the law of multiplication twice the number. But it is not so exact as that, nor so self-evident. When we are dealing with men, our ready-reckoner rules do not work out correctly. In this region one and one are not always two. They are sometimes more than two, and sometimes less than two. Union of all kinds, which may be strength, may be weakness. It was not till Gideon weeded out his army, once and twice, that he was promised victory. The fruits of friendship may be corrupting, and unspeakably evil to the life. The reward of the labor of two may be less than that of one.

66

Friendship

The boy pulling a barrow is lucky if he
get another boy to shove behind, but if the
boy behind not only ceases to shove, but
sits on the barrow, the last end is worse
than the first.   A threefold cord with two
of the strands rotten is worse than a single
sound strand, for it deceives into putting
too much weight on it.

In social economics it is evident that
society is not merely the sum of the units
that compose it.   Two are better than
one, not merely because the force is
doubled.   It may even be said that two
are better than two.   Two together mean
more than two added singly ; for a new
element is introduced which increases the
power of each individually.   When the
man Friday came into the life of Rob-
inson Crusoe, he brought with him a
great deal more than his own individual
value, which with his lower civilization
would not be very much.   But to Rob-
inson Crusoe he represented society, and
all the possibilities of social polity.   It

meant also the satisfaction of the social instincts, the play of the affections, and made Crusoe a different man. The two living together were more than the two living on different desert islands.

The truth of this strange contradiction of the multiplication table is seen in the relationship of friends. Each gives to the other, and each receives, and the fruit of the intercourse is more than either in himself possesses. Every individual relationship has contact with a universal. To reach out to the fuller life of love is a divine enchantment, because it leads to more than itself, and is the open door into the mystery of life. We feel ourselves united to the race and no longer isolated units, but in the sweep of the great social forces which mould mankind. Every bond which binds man to man is a new argument for the permanence of life itself, and gives a new insight into its meaning. Love is the pledge and the promise of the future.

Friendship

Besides this cosmic and perhaps somewhat shadowy benefit, there are many practical fruits of friendship to the individual. These may be classified and subdivided almost endlessly, and indeed in every special friendship the fruits of it will differ according to the character and closeness of the tie, and according to the particular gifts of each of the partners. One man can give to his friend some quality of sympathy, or some kind of help, or can supply some social need which is lacking in his character or circumstances. Perhaps it is not possible to get a better division of the subject than the three noble fruits of friendship which Bacon enumerates — peace in the affections, support of the judgment, and aid in all actions and occasions.

First of all there is the *satisfaction of the heart*. We cannot live a self-centred life, without feeling that we are missing the true glory of life. We were made for social intercourse, if only that the highest qualities of our nature might have an opportunity for development. The joy, which a true friendship gives, reveals the existence of the want of it, perhaps previously unfelt. It is a sin against ourselves to let our affections wither. This sense of incompleteness is an argument in favor of its possible satisfaction; our need is an argument for its fulfilment. Our hearts demand love, as truly as our bodies demand food. We cannot live among men, suspicious, and careful of our own interests, and fighting for our own hand, without doing dishonor and hurt to our own nature. To be for ourselves puts the whole world against us. To harden our heart hardens the heart of the universe.

We need sympathy, and therefore we crave for friendship. Even the most perfect of the sons of men felt this need of intercourse of the heart. Christ, in one aspect the most self-contained of men,

Friendship

showed this human longing all through His life. He ever desired opportunities for enlargement of heart — in His disciples, in an inner circle within the circle, in the household of Bethany. " Will ye also go away?" He asked in the crisis of His career. " Could ye not watch with Me one hour?" He sighed in His great agony. He was perfectly human, and therefore felt the lack of friendship. The higher our relationships with each other are, the closer is the intercourse demanded. Highest of all in the things of the soul, we feel that the true Christian life cannot be lived in the desert, but must be a life among men, and this because it is a life of joy as well as of service. We feel that, for the rounding of our life and the completion of our powers, we need intercourse with our kind. Stunted affections dwarf the whole man. We live by admiration, hope, and love, and these can be developed only in the social life.

71

The sweetest and most stable pleasures also are never selfish. They are derived from fellowship, from common tastes, and mutual sympathy. Sympathy is not a quality merely needed in adversity. It is needed as much when the sun shines. Indeed, it is more easily obtained in adversity than in prosperity. It is comparatively easy to sympathize with a friend's *failure*, when we are not so true-hearted about his success. When a man is down in his luck, he can be sure of at least a certain amount of good-fellowship to which he can appeal. It is difficult to keep a little touch of malice, or envy, out of congratulations. It is sometimes easier to weep with those who weep, than to rejoice with those who rejoice. This difficulty is felt not with people above us, or with little connection with us, but with our equals. When a friend succeeds, there may be a certain regret which has not always an evil root, but is due to a fear that he is getting beyond our reach, passing out of our sphere, and perhaps will not need or desire our friendship so much as before. It is a dangerous feeling to give way to, but up to a certain point is natural and legitimate. A perfect friendship would not have room for such grudging sympathy, but would rejoice more for the other's success than for his own. The envious, jealous man never can be a friend. His mean spirit of detraction and insinuating ill-will kills friendship at its birth. Plutarch records a witty remark about Plistarchus, who was told that a notorious railer had spoken well of him. "I'll lay my life," said he, "somebody has told him I am dead, for he can speak well of no man living."

For true satisfaction of the heart, there must be a fount of sympathy from which to draw in all the vicissitudes of life. Sorrow asks for sympathy, aches to let its griefs be known and shared by a kindred spirit. To find such, is to dispel the loneliness from life. To have a heart which we can trust, and into which we can pour our griefs and our doubts and our fears, is already to take the edge from grief, and the sting from doubt, and the shade from fear.

Joy also demands that its joy should be shared. The man who has found his sheep that was lost calls together his neighbors, and bids them rejoice with him because he has found the sheep that was lost. Joy is more social than grief. Some forms of grief desire only to creep away into solitude like a wounded beast to its lair, to suffer alone and to die alone. But joy finds its counterpart in the sunshine and the flowers and the birds and the little children, and enters easily into all the movements of life. Sympathy will respond to a friend's gladness, as well as vibrate to his grief. A simple generous friendship will thus add to the joy, and will divide the sorrow.

The religious life, in spite of all the un-

74

Friendship

natural experiments of monasticism and all its kindred ascetic forms, is preëminently a life of friendship. It is individual in its root, and social in its fruits. It is when two or three are gathered together that religion becomes a fact for the world. The joy of religion will not be hid and buried in a man's own heart. "Come, see a man that told me all that ever I did," is the natural outcome of the first wonder and the first faith. It spreads from soul to soul by the impact of soul on soul, from the original impact of the great soul of God.

Christ's ideal is the ideal of a Kingdom, men banded together in a common cause, under common laws, serving the same purpose of love. It is meant to take effect upon man in all his social relationships, in the home, in the city, in the state. Its greatest triumphs have been made through friendship, and it in turn has ennobled and sanctified the bond. The growth of the Kingdom depends on

the sanctified working of the natural ties
among men. It was so at the very start :
John the Baptist pointed out the Christ
to John the future Apostle and to Andrew ; Andrew findeth his own brother
Simon Peter ; Philip findeth Nathanael ;
and so society through its network of
relations took into its heart the new
message. The man who has been healed
must go and tell those who are at home,
must declare it to his friends, and seek
that they also should share in his great
discovery.

The very existence of the Church as a
body of believers is due to this necessity
of our nature, which demands opportunity for the interchange of Christian
sentiment. The deeper the feeling, the
greater is the joy of sharing it with
another. There is a strange felicity, a
wondrous enchantment, which comes from
true intimacy of heart, and close communion of soul, and the result is more
than mere fleeting joy. When it is

Friendship

shared in the deepest thoughts and highest aspirations, when it is built on a common faith, and lives by a common hope, it brings perfect peace. No friendship has done its work until it reaches the supremest satisfaction of spiritual communion.

Besides this satisfaction of the heart, friendship also gives *satisfaction of the mind*. Most men have a certain natural diffidence in coming to conclusions and forming opinions for themselves. We rarely feel confident, until we have secured the agreement of others in whom we trust. There is always a personal equation in all our judgments, so that we feel that they require to be amended by comparison with those of others. Doctors ask for a consultation, when a case becomes critical. We all realize the advantage of taking counsel. To ask for advice is a benefit, whether we follow the advice or no. Indeed, the best benefit often comes from the opportunity of testing our own opinion and finding it valid. Sometimes the very statement of the case is enough to prove it one thing or the other. An advantage is reaped from a sympathetic listener, even although our friend be unable to elucidate the matter by his special sagacity or experience. Friends in counsel gain much intellectually. They acquire something approaching to a standard of judgment, and are enabled to classify opinions, and to make up the mind more accurately and securely. Through talking a subject over with another, one gets fresh side-lights into it, new avenues open up, and the whole question becomes larger and richer. Bacon says, "Friendship maketh daylight in the understanding, out of darkness and confusion of thoughts: neither is this to be understood only of faithful counsel, which a man receiveth from his friend; but before you come to that, certain it is, that whosoever hath his mind fraught with many thoughts, his wits and un-

derstanding do clarify and break up in
the communicating and discoursing with
another; he tosseth his thoughts more
easily; he marshalleth them more or-
derly; he seeth how they look when they
are turned into words; finally he wax-
eth wiser than himself; and that more
by an hour's discourse than by a day's
meditation."

We must have been struck with the
brilliancy of our own conversation and
the profundity of our own thoughts,
when we shared them with one, with
whom we were in sympathy at the time.
The brilliancy was not ours; it was the
reflex action which was the result of the
communion. That is why the effect of
different people upon us is different, one
making us creep into our shell and making us unable almost to utter a word; another through some strange magnetism
enlarging the bounds of our whole being
and drawing the best out of us. The
true insight after all is love. It clarifies

the intellect, and opens the eyes to much that was obscure.

Besides the subjective influence, there may be the great gain of honest counsel. A faithful friend can be trusted not to speak merely soft words of flattery. It is often the spectator who sees most of the game, and, if the spectator is at the same time keenly interested in us, he can have a more unbiased opinion than we can possibly have. He may have to say that which may wound our self-esteem; he may have to speak for correction rather than for commendation; but "Faithful are the wounds of a friend." The flatterer will take good care not to offend our susceptibilities by too many shocks of wholesome truth-telling; but a friend will seek our good, even if he must say the thing we hate to hear at the time.

This does not mean that a friend should always be what is called plain-spoken. Many take advantage of what they call

Friendship

a true interest in our welfare, in order to
rub gall into our wounds. The man who
boasts of his frankness and of his hatred
of flattery, is usually not frank — but
only brutal. A true friend will never
needlessly hurt, but also will never let
slip occasions through cowardice. To
speak the truth in love takes off the
edge of unpleasantness, which so often
is found in truth-speaking. And however the wound may smart, in the end
we are thankful for the faithfulness which
caused it. " Let the righteous smite me ;
it shall be a kindness : and let him re-
prove me ; it shall be an excellent oil,
which shall not break my head."

In our relations with each other, there
is usually more advantage to be reaped
from friendly encouragement, than from
friendly correction. True criticism does
not consist, as so many critics seem to
think, in depreciation, but in appreciation ; in putting oneself sympathetically
in another's position, and seeking to value

the real worth of his work. <u>There are
more lives spoiled by undue harshness,
than by undue gentleness.</u> More good
work is lost from want of appreciation
than from too much of it ; and certainly
it is not the function of friendship to do
the critic's work. Unless carefully re-
pressed, such a spirit becomes censorious,
or, worse still, spiteful, and has often
been the means of losing a friend. It
is possible to be kind, without giving
crooked counsel, or oily flattery ; and it
is possible to be true, without magnifying
faults, and indulging in cruel rebukes.

Besides the joy of friendship, and its
aid in matters of counsel, a third of its
noble fruits is the direct *help* it can give
us in the difficulties of life. It gives
strength to the character. It sobers and
steadies through the responsibility for
each other which it means. When men
face the world together, and are ready to
stand shoulder to shoulder, the sense of

Friendship

comradeship makes each strong. This
help may not often be called into play,
but just to know that it is there if needed
is a great comfort, to know that if one
fall the other will lift him up. The very
word friendship suggests kindly help and
aid in distress. Shakespeare applies the
word in *King Lear* to an inanimate thing
with this meaning of helpfulness, —

Gracious my lord, hard by here is a hovel ;
Some *friendship* will it lend you 'gainst the
   tempest.

Sentiment does not amount to much, if
it is not an inspiring force to lead to gentle and to generous deeds, when there is
need. The fight is not so hard, when we
know that we are not alone, but that
there are some who think of us, and pray
for us, and would gladly help us if they
got the opportunity.

Comradeship is one of the finest facts,
and one of the strongest forces in life. A
mere strong man, however capable, and

however singly successful, is of little account by himself. There is no glamour of romance in his career. The kingdom of Romance belongs to David, not to Samson — to David, with his eager, impetuous, affectionate nature, for whom three men went in the jeopardy of life to bring him a drink of water; and all for love of him. It is not the self-centred, self-contained hero, who lays hold of us; it is ever the comradeship of heroes. Dumas' Three Musketeers (and the Gascon who made a greater fourth), with their oath, " Each for all, and all for each," inherit that kingdom of Romance, with all that ever have been tied in bands of love.

Robertson of Brighton in one of his letters tells how a friend of his had, through cowardice or carelessness, missed an opportunity of putting him right on a point with which he was charged, and so left him defenceless against a slander. With his native sweetness of soul, he contents himself with the exclamation, " How rare

Friendship

it is to have a friend who will defend you
thoroughly and boldly!" Yet that is just
one of the loyal things a friend can do,
sometimes when it would be impossible
for a man himself to do himself justice
with others. Some things, needful to be
said or done under certain circumstances,
cannot be undertaken without indelicacy
by the person concerned, and the keen
instinct of a friend should tell him that
he is needed. A little thoughtfulness
would often suggest things that could be
done for our friends, that would make
them feel that the tie which binds us to
them is a real one. That man is rich indeed, who possesses thoughtful, tactful
friends, with whom he feels safe when
present, and in whose hands his honor is
secure when absent. If there be no loyalty, there can be no great friendship.
Most of our friendships lack the distinction of greatness, because we are not
ready for little acts of service. Without
these our love dwindles down to a mere

sentiment, and ceases to be the inspiring
force for good to both lives, which it was
at the beginning.

The aid we may receive from friendship may be of an even more powerful,
because of a more subtle, nature than
material help. It may be a safeguard
against temptation. The recollection of
a friend whom we admire is a great force
to save us from evil, and to prompt us
to good. The thought of his sorrow in
any moral break-down of ours will often
nerve us to stand firm. What would my
friend think of me, if I did this, or con-
sented to this meanness? Could I look
him in the face again, and meet the calm
pure gaze of his eye? Would it not be
a blot on our friendship, and draw a veil
over our intercourse? No friendship is
worth the name which does not elevate,
and does not help to nobility of conduct
and to strength of character. It should
give a new zest to duty, and a new inspiration to all that is good.

86

Friendship

Influence is the greatest of all human gifts, and we all have it in some measure. There are some to whom we are something, if not everything. There are some, who are grappled to us with hoops of steel. There are some, over whom we have ascendency, or at least to whom we have access, who have opened the gates of the City of Mansoul to us, some we can sway with a word, a touch, a look. It must always be a solemn thing for a man to ask what he has done with this dread power of influence. For what has our friend to be indebted to us — for good or for evil? Have we put on his armor, and sent him out with courage and strength to the battle? Or have we dragged him down from the heights to which he once aspired? We are face to face here with the tragic possibilities of human intercourse. In all friendship we open the gates of the city, and those who have entered must be either allies in the fight, or treacherous foes.

Friendship

All the fruits of friendship, be they blessed or baneful, spring from this root of influence, and influence in the long run is the impress of our real character on other lives. Influence cannot rise above the level of our lives. The result of our friendship on others will ultimately be conditioned by the sort of persons we are. It adds a very sacred responsibility to life. Here, as in other regions, a good tree bringeth forth good fruit, but a corrupt tree bringeth forth evil fruit.

The Choice of
Friendship

*IF thou findest a good man, rise up early in the
morning to go to him, and let thy feet wear the
steps of his door.*

THE APOCRYPHAL BOOK OF ECCLESIASTICUS.

*Whereof the man, that with me trod
This planet, was a noble type,
Appearing ere the times were ripe,
That friend of mine who lives with God.*

TENNYSON.

The
Choice of
Friendship

OUR responsibility for our friendships is not confined to making
sure that our influence over others
is for good. We have also a duty to ourselves. As we possess the gift of influence
over others, so we in turn are affected by
every life which touches ours. Influence
is like an atmosphere exhaled by each
separate personality. Some men seem
neutral and colorless, with no atmosphere
to speak of. Some have a bad atmosphere,
like the rank poisonous odor of noxious
weeds, breeding malaria. If our moral
sense were only keen and true, we would
instinctively know them, as some children
do, and dread their company. Others
have a good atmosphere ; we can breathe
there in safety, and have a joyful sense of
security. With some of these it is a local

delicate environment, sweet, suggestive, like the aroma of wild violets : we have to look, and sometimes to stoop, to get into its range. With some it is like a pine forest, or a eucalyptus grove of warmer climes, which perfumes a whole country side. It is well to know such, Christ's little ones and Christ's great ones. They put oxygen into the moral atmosphere, and we breathe more freely for it. They give us new insight, and fresh courage, and purer faith, and by the impulse of their example inspire us to nobler life.

There is nothing so important as the choice of friendship ; for it both reflects character and affects it. A man is known by the company he keeps. This is an infallible test ; for his thoughts, and desires, and ambitions, and loves are revealed here. He gravitates naturally to his congenial sphere. And it affects character ; for it is the atmosphere he breathes. It enters his blood and makes the circuit of his veins. " All love assimilates to what

Friendship

it loves." A man is moulded into likeness of the lives that come nearest him. It is at the point of the emotions that he i̇ most impressionable. The material surroundings, the outside lot of a man, affects him, but after all that is mostly on the outside ; for the higher functions of life may be served in almost any external circumstances. But the environment of other lives, the communion of other souls, are far more potent facts. The nearer people are to each other, and the less disguise there is in their relationship, the more invariably will the law of spiritual environment act.

It seems a tragedy that people, who see each other as they are, become like each other ; and often it is a tragedy. But the law carries as much hope in it as despair. If through it evil works havoc, through it also good persists. If we are hindered by the weakness of our associates, we are often helped by their goodness and sweetness. Contact with a strong nature inspires us with strength. Some one once asked Kingsley what was the secret of his strong joyous life, and he answered, "I had a friend." If every evil man is a centre of contagion, every good man is a centre of healing. He provides an environment in which others can see God. Goodness creates an atmosphere for other souls to be good. It is a priestly garment that has virtue even for the finger that touches it. The earth has its salt, and the world has its light, in the sweet souls, and winsome lives, and Christ-like characters to be found in it. The choice of friends is therefore one of the most serious affairs in life, just because a man becomes moulden into the likeness of what he loves in his friend.

From the purely selfish standard, every fresh tie we form means giving a new hostage to fortune, and adding a new risk to our happiness. Apart from any moral evil, every intimacy is a danger of another blow to the heart. But if we desire fulness of life, we cannot help ourselves. A man may make many a friendship to his own hurt, but the isolated life is a greater danger still. *Societas est mater discordiarum*, which Scott in his humorous pathetic account of the law-suits of Peter Peebles *versus* Plainstanes in " Redgauntlet," translates, Partnership oft makes pleaship. Every relationship means risk, but we must take the risk ; for while nearly all our sorrows come from our connection with others, nearly all our joys have the same source. We cannot help ourselves ; for it is part of the great discipline of life. Rather, we need knowledge, and care, and forethought to enable us to make the best use of the necessities of our nature. And foremost of these for importance is our choice of friends.

We may err on the one side by being too cautious, and too exclusive in our attachments. We may be supercilious, and disdainful in our estimate of men. Contempt always blinds the eyes. Every man is vulnerable somewhere, if only like Achilles in the heel. The true secret of insight is not contempt, but sympathy. Such disdain usually means putting all the eggs into one basket, when a smash spells ruin.

The other extreme is the attitude, which easily makes many friends, without much consideration of quality. We know the type of man, who is friendly with everybody, and a friend of none. He is Hail fellow well met! with every passing stranger, a boon companion of every wayfarer. He takes up with every sort of casual comrade, and seeks to be on good terms with everybody. He makes what is called, with a little contempt, good company, and is a favorite on all light occasions. His affections spread themselves out over a large expanse. He is easily consoled for a loss, and easily attracted by a new attachment. And as he deals, so is he dealt with. Many like him; few quite trust him. He makes

many friends, and is not particular about
their quality. The law of spiritual environment plays upon him with its relentless force. He gives himself away too
cheaply, and opens himself to all sorts
of influence. He is constantly laying
himself in the way of temptation. His
mind takes on the opinions of his set: his
character assimilates itself to the forces
that act on it. The evil example of
some of his intimates gradually breaks
down the barriers of past training and
teaching. The desire to please a crowd
means that principle is let slip, and conscience ceases to be the standard of action. His very friends are not true
friends, being mostly of the fair-weather
quality.

Though it may seem difficult to avoid
either of these two extremes, it will not
do to refuse to choose at all, and leave
things to chance. We drift into many
of our connections with men, but the art
of seamanship is tested by sailing not by

drifting. The subject of the choice of friendship is not advanced much by just letting them choose us. That is to become the victim, not the master of our circumstances. And while it is true that we are acted on as much as we act, and are chosen as much as we choose, it is not permitted to any one merely to be passive, except at great cost.

At the same time in the mystery of friendship we cannot say that we went about with a touchstone testing all we met, till we found the ore that would respond to our particular magnet. It is not that we said to ourselves, Go to, we will choose a friend, and straightway made a distinct election to the vacant throne of our heart. From one point of view we were absolutely passive. Things arranged themselves without effort, and by some subtle affinity we learned that we had gained a friend. The history of every true friendship is the brief description of Emerson, " My friends have come

Friendship

to me unsought ; the great God gave them to me." There was an element of necessity in this, as in all crises of life.

Does it therefore seem absurd and useless to speak about the choice of friendship at all ? By no means, because the principles we set before ourselves will determine the kind of friends we have, as truly as if the whole initiative lay with us. We are chosen for the same reason for which we would choose. To try to separate the two processes is to make the same futile distinction, on a lower scale, so often made between choosing God and being chosen by Him. It is futile, because the distinction cannot be maintained.

Besides, the value of having some definite principle by which to test friendship is not confined to the positive attachments made. The necessity for a system of selection is largely due to the necessity for rejection. The good and great intimacies of our life will perhaps come to

us, as the wind bloweth, we cannot tell
how. But by regulating our course
wisely, we will escape from hampering
our life by mistakes, and weakening it
with false connections. We ought to be
courteous, and kind, and gentle with all,
but not to all can we open the sanctuary
of our heart.

We have a graduated scale of intimacy,
from introduction, and nodding acquaintance, and speaking acquaintance,
through an endless series of kinds
of intercourse to the perfect friendship.
In counting up our gains and our re-
sources, we cannot give them all the same
value, without deceiving ourselves. To
expect loyalty and devotion from all alike
is to court disappointment. Most mis-
anthropical and cynical estimates of man
are due to this mingled ignorance and
conceit. We cannot look for undying
affection from the crowd we may happen
to have entertained to dinner, or have
rubbed shoulders with at business resorts

or at social gatherings. Many men in life, as many are depicted in literature, have played the misanthrope, because they have discovered through adversity how many of their associates were fair-weather friends. In their prosperity they encouraged toadying and sycophancy. They liked to have hangers-on, who would flatter, and when the east wind blows they are indignant that their circle should prefer to avoid it.

Shakespeare's Timon of Athens is a typical misanthrope in his virtuous indignation at the cat-like love of men for comfort. In his prosperity crowds of glass-faced flatterers bent before him, and were made rich in Timon's nod. He wasted his substance in presents and hospitality, and bred a fine race of parasites and trencher-friends. When he spent all and began to be in want, no man gave unto him. The winter shower drove away the summer flies. He had loved the reputation for splendid liberality, and lavish generosity, and had sought to be a little god among men, bestowing favors and receiving homage, all of which was only a more subtle form of selfishness. When the brief day of prosperity passed, men shut their doors against the setting sun. The smooth and smilling crowd dropped off with a shrug, and Timon went to the other extreme of misanthropy, declaimed against friendship, and cursed men for their ingratitude. But after all he got what he had paid for. He thought he had been buying the hearts of men, and found that he had only bought their mouths, and tongues, and eyes.

"He that loves to be flattered is worthy of the flatterer." For moral value there is not much to choose between them. Rats are said to desert the sinking ship, which is not to be wondered at in rats. The choice of friendship does not mean the indiscriminate acceptance of all who are willing to assume the name of friend.

102

Friendship

A touch of east wind is good, not only to weed out the false and test the true, but also to brace a man to the stern realities of life. When we find that some of our intimates are dispersed by adversity, instead of raving against the world's ingratitude like Timon, we should be glad that now we know whom exactly we can trust.

Another common way of choosing friends, and one which also meets with its own fitting reward, is the selfish method of valuing men according to their usefulness to us. To add to their credit, or reputation, some are willing to include anybody in their list of intimates. For business purposes even, men will sometimes run risks, by endangering the peace of their home and the highest interests of those they love; they are ready to introduce into their family circle men whom they distrust morally, because they think they can make some gain out of the connection.

All the stupid snobbishness, and mean tuft-hunting so common, are due to the same desire to make use of people in some way or other. It is an abuse of the word friendship to apply it to such social scrambling. Of course, even tuft-hunting may be only a perverted desire after what we think the best, a longing to get near those we consider of nobler nature and larger mind than common associates. It may be an instinctive agreement with Plato's definition of the wise man, as ever wanting to be with him who is better than himself. But in its usual form it becomes an unspeakable degradation, inducing servility, and lick-spittle humility, and all the vices of the servile mind. There can never be true friendship without self-respect, and unless soul meets soul free from self-seeking. If we had higher standards for ourselves, if we lived to God and not to men, we would also find that in the truest sense we would live with men.

Friendship

We need not go out of our way to ingratiate ourselves with anybody. Nothing can make up for the loss of independence and native dignity of soul. It is not for a man, made in the image of God, to grovel, and demean himself before his fellow creatures.

After all it defeats itself; for there can only be friendship *between equals*. This does not mean equals in what is called social position, nor even in intellectual attainments, though these naturally have weight, but it means equality which has a spiritual source. Can two walk together, except they be agreed? Nor does it mean identity, nor even likeness. Indeed, for the highest unity there must be difference, the difference of free beings, with will, and conscience, and mind unhampered. We often make much of our differences, forgetting that really we differ, and *can* differ, only because we agree. Without many points of contact, there could be no divergence from these.

Argument and contradiction of opinion
are the outcome of difference, and yet
for argument there is needed a common
basis. We cannot even discuss, unless
we meet on some mental ground common to both disputants. So there may
be, nay, for the highest union there must
be, a great general conformity behind the
distinctions, a deep underlying common
basis beneath the unlikeness. And for
true union of hearts, this equality must
have a spiritual source. If then there
must be some spiritual affinity, agreement in what is best and highest in each,
we can see the futility of most of the
selfish attempts to make capital out of
our intercourse. Our friends will be, because they must be, our equals. We can
never have a nobler intimacy, until we
are made fit for it.

All connections based on selfishness,
either on personal pleasure or on usefulness, are accidental. They are easily
dissolved, because, when the pleasure

or the utility ceases, the bond ceases. When the motive of the friendship is removed, the friendship itself disappears. The perfect friendship is grounded on what is permanent, on goodness, on character. It is of much slower growth, since it takes some time to really find out the truly lovable things in a life, but it is lasting, since the foundation is stable.

The most important point, then, about the choice of friendship is that we should know what to reject. Countless attractions come to us on the lower plane. A man may be attracted by what his own conscience tells him to be unworthy. He may have slipped gradually into companionship with some, whose influence is even evil. He may have got, almost without his own will, into a set which is deteriorating his life and character. He knows the fruits of his weakness, in the lowering of the moral tone, in the slackening grip of the conscience, in the looser flow of the blood. He has become pliant in will, feeble in purpose, and flaccid in character. Every man has a duty to himself to be his own best self, and he can never be that under the spell of evil companionship.

Some men mix in doubtful company, and say that they have no Pharisaic exclusiveness, and even sometimes defend themselves by Christ's example, who received sinners and ate with them. The comparison borders on blasphemy. It depends on the purpose, for which sinners are received. Christ never joined in their sin, but went to save them from their sin; and wickedness could not lift its head in His presence. Some seek to be initiated into the mysteries of iniquity, in idle or morbid curiosity, perhaps to write a realistic book, or to see life, as it is called. There is often a prurient desire to explore the tracts of sin, as if information on such subjects meant wisdom. If men are honest with themselves, they will admit that they join the

company of sinners, for the relish they
have for the sin. We must first obey
the moral command to come out from
among them and be separate, before it is
possible for us to meet them like Christ.
Separateness of soul is the law of holi-
ness. Of Christ, of whom it was said that
this man receiveth sinners, it was also said
that He was separate from sinners. The
knowledge of wickedness is not wisdom,
neither is the counsel of sinners prudence.
Most young men know the temptation
here referred to, the curiosity to learn
the hidden things, and to have the air of
those who know the world.

If we have gone wrong here, and have
admitted into the sanctuary of our lives
influences that make for evil, we must
break away from them at all costs. The
sweeter and truer relationships of our
life should arm us for the struggle, the
prayers of a mother, the sorrow of true
friends. This is the fear, countless times,
in the hearts of the folks at home when

their boy leaves them to win his way in
the city, the deadly fear lest he should
fall into evil habits, and into the clutches
of evil men. They know that there are
men whose touch, whose words, whose
very look, is contamination. To give
them entrance into our lives is to submit ourselves to the contagion of sin.

Friends should be chosen by a higher
principle of selection than any worldly
one, of pleasure, or usefulness, or by weak
submission to the evil influences of our
lot. They should be chosen for character, for goodness, for truth and trust-
worthiness, because they have sympathy
with us in our best thoughts and holiest
aspirations, because they have community of mind in the things of the soul.
All other connections are fleeting and
imperfect from the nature of the case.
A relationship based on the physical
withers when the first bloom fades : a
relationship founded on the intellectual
is only a little more secure, as it too is

Friendship

subject to caprice. All purely earthly partnerships, like all earthly treasures, are exposed to decay, the bite of the moth and the stain of the rust; and they must all have an end.

A young man may get opposing advice from two equally trusted counsellors. One will advise him to cultivate the friendship of the clever, because they will afterward occupy places of power in the world: the other will advise him to cultivate the friendship of the good, because if they do not inherit the earth, they aspire to the heavens. If he knows the character of the two counsellors, he will understand why they should look upon life from such different standpoints; and later on he will find that while some of his friends were both clever and good, not one of the purely intellectual friendships remains to him. It does not afford a sufficient basis of agreement, to stand the tear and wear of life. The basis of friendship must be community of soul.

111

Friendship

The only permanent severance of heart comes through lack of a common spiritual footing. If one soul goes up the mountain top, and the other stays down among the shadows, if the two have not the same high thoughts, and pure desires, and ideals of service, they cannot remain together except in form. Friends need not be identical in temperament and capacity, but they must be alike in sympathy. An unequal yoke becomes either an intolerable burden, or will drag one of the partners away from the path his soul at its best would have loved to tread.

If you loved only what were worth your love,
Love were clear gain, and wholly well for you.

If we choose our friends in Christ, neither here, nor ever, need we fear parting, and will have the secure joy and peace which come from having a friend who is as one's own soul.

The Eclipse of
Friendship

*F*OR Lycidas is dead, dead ere his prime,
    Young Lycidas, and hath not left his peer.

   ·   ·   ·   ·   ·

Weep no more, woeful shepherds, weep no more
For Lycidas, your sorrow, is not dead.
Sunk though he be beneath the watery floor.
So sinks the day-star in the ocean bed,
And yet anon repairs his drooping head,
And tricks his beams, and with new-spangled ore
Flames in the forehead of the morning sky:
So Lycidas sunk low, but mounted high,
Through the dear might of Him that walked the waves.

                      MILTON.

The Eclipse of Friendship

AS it is one of the greatest joys of
life when a kindred soul is for the
first time recognized and claimed,
so it is one of the bitterest moments of
life when the first rupture is made of the
ties which bind us to other lives. Before
it comes, it is hard to believe that it is
possible, if we ever think of it at all.
When it does come, it is harder still to
understand the meaning of the blow. The
miracle of friendship seemed too fair, to
carry in its bosom the menace of its loss.
We knew, of course, that such things had
been, and must be, but we never quite
realized what it would be to be the victims of the common doom of man.

If it only came as a sudden pain, that
passes after its brief spasm of agony, it
would not be so sore an affliction; but

115

when it comes, it comes to stay. There remains a place in our hearts which is tender to every touch, and it is touched so often. We survive the shock of the moment easier than the constant reminder of our loss. The old familiar face, debarred to the sense of sight, can be recalled by a stray word, a casual sight, a chance memory. The closer the intercourse had been, the more things there are in our lives associated with him — things that we did together, places that we visited together, thoughts even that we thought together.

There seems no region of life where we can escape from the suggestions of memory. The sight of any little object can bring him back, with his way of speaking, with his tricks of gesture, with all the qualities for which we loved him, and for which we mourn him now. If the intimacy was due to mere physical proximity, the loss will be only a vague sense of uneasiness through the breakdown of long-

Friendship

continued habit; but, if the two lives were woven into the same web, there must be ragged edges left, and it is a weary task to take up the threads again, and find a new woof for the warp. The closer the connection has been, the keener is the loss. It comes back to us at the sight of the many things associated with him, and, fill up our lives with countless distractions as we may, the shadow creeps back to darken the world.

Sometimes there is the added pain of remorse that we did not enough appreciate the treasure we possessed. In thoughtlessness we accepted the gift; we had so little idea of the true value of his friendship; we loved so little, and were so impatient :— if only we had him back again; if only we had one more opportunity to show him how dear he was; if only we had another chance of proving ourselves worthy. We can hardly forgive ourselves that we were so cold and selfish. Self-reproach, the regret of the unaccepted opportunity, is one of the commonest feelings after bereavement, and it is one of the most blessed.

Still, it may become a morbid feeling. It is a false sentimentalism which lives in the past, and lavishes its tenderness on memory. It is difficult to say what is the dividing line between healthy sorrow and morbid sentiment. It seems a natural instinct, which makes the bereaved care lovingly for the very grave, and which makes the mother keep locked up the little shoes worn by the little feet, relics hid from the vulgar eye. The instinct has become a little more morbid, when it has preserved the room of a dead mother, with its petty decorations and ornaments as she left them. Beautiful as the instinct may be, there is nothing so dangerous as when our most natural feeling turns morbid.

It is always a temptation, which grows stronger the longer we live, to look back

118

Friendship

instead of forward, to bemoan the past, and thus deride the present and distrust the future. We must not forget our present blessings, the love we still possess, the gracious influences that remain, and most of all the duties that claim our strength. The loving women who went early in the morning to the sepulchre of the buried Christ were met with a rebuke, "Why seek ye the living among the dead?" They were sent back to life to find Him, and sent back to life to do honor to His death. Not by ointments and spices, however precious, nor at the rock-hewn tomb, could they best remember their Lord; but out in the world, which that morning had seemed so cold and cheerless, and in their lives, which then had seemed not worth living.

Christianity does not condemn any natural human feeling, but it will not let these interfere with present duty and destroy future usefulness. It does not send men to search for the purpose of living in the

graves of their dead hopes and pleasures.
Its disciples must not attempt to live on
the relics of even great incidents, among
crucifixes and tombs. In the Desert, the
heart must reach forward to the Promised Land, and not back to Egypt. The
Christian faith is for the future, because
it believes in the God of the future. The
world is not a lumber room, full of relics
and remembrances, over which to brood.
We are asked to remember the beautiful
past which was ours, and the beautiful
lives which we have lost, by making the
present beautiful like it, and our lives
beautiful like theirs. It is human to think
that life has no future, if now it seems
"dark with griefs and graves." It comes
like a shock to find that we must bury
our sorrow, and come into contact with
the hard world again, and live our common life once more. The Christian learns
to do it, not because he has a short memory, but because he has a long faith.
The voice of inspiration is heard oftener

Friendship

through the realities of life, than through
vain regrets and recluse dreams. The
Christian life must be in its degree something like the Master's own life, lumi-
nous with His hope, and surrounded by
a bracing atmosphere which uplifts all
who even touch its outer fringe.

The great fact of life, nevertheless, is
death, and it must have a purpose to
serve and a lesson to teach. It seems to
lose something of its impressiveness, because it is universal. The very inevitableness of it seems to kill thought,
rather than induce it. It is only when
the blow strikes home, that we are pulled
up and forced to face the fact. Theo-
retically there is a wonderful unanimity
among men, regarding the shortness of
life and the uncertainty of all human relationships. The last word of the wise
on life has ever been its fleetingness, its
appalling changes, its unexpected sur-
prises. The only certainty of life is its

uncertainty — its unstable tenure, its inevitable end. But practically we go on as if we could lay our plans, and mortgage time, without doubt or danger; until cur feet are knocked from under us by some sudden shock, and we realize how unstable the equilibrium of life really is. The lesson of life is death.

The experience would not be so tragically universal, if it had not a good and necessary meaning. For one thing it should sober us, and make our lives full of serious, solemn purpose. It should teach us to number our days that we may apply our hearts to wisdom. The man, who has no place for death in his philosophy, has not learned to live. The lesson of death is life.

On the whole, however, it is not our own liability to death which oppresses us. The fear of it to a brave man, not to speak of a man of faith, can be overcome. It is the fear of it *for others* whom we love, which is its sting. And

Friendship

none of us can live very long without
knowing in our own heart's experience
the reality, as well as the terror, of death.
This too has its meaning for us, to look
at life more tenderly, and touch it more
gently. The pathos of life is only a
forced sentiment to us, if we have not
felt the pity of life. To a sensitive soul,
smarting with his own loss, the world
sometimes seems full of graves, and for
a time at least makes him walk softly
among men.

This is one reason why the making of
new friends is so much easier in youth
than later on. Friendship comes to youth
seemingly without any conditions, and
without any fears. There is no past to
look back at, with much regret and some
sorrow. We never look behind us, *till
we miss something*. Youth is satisfied
with the joy of present possession. To
the young friendship comes as the glory
of spring, a very miracle of beauty, a
mystery of birth : to the old it has the

bloom of autumn, beautiful still, but with the beauty of decay. To the young it is chiefly hope: to the old it is mostly memory. The man who is conscious that he has lost the best of his days, the best of his powers, the best of his friends, naturally lives a good deal in the past.

Such a man is prepared for further losses; he has adjusted himself to the fact of death. At first, we cannot believe that it can happen to us and to our love; or, if the thought comes to us, it is an event too far in the future to ruffle the calm surface of our heart. And yet, it must come; from it none can escape. Most can remember a night of waiting, too stricken for prayer, too numb of heart even for feeling, vaguely expecting the blow to strike us out of the dark. A strange sense of the unreality of things came over us, when the black wave submerged us and passed on. We went out into the sunshine, and it seemed to

Friendship

mock us. We entered again among the
busy ways of men, and the roar of life
beat upon our brain and heart,

> Yet in these ears, till hearing dies,
> One set slow bell will seem to toll,
> The passing of the sweetest soul
> That ever looked with human eyes.

Was it worth while to have linked our
lives on to other lives, and laid ourselves
open to such desolation? Would it not
be better to go through the world, without joining ourselves too closely to the
fleeting bonds of other loves? Why de-
liberately add to our disabilities? But
it is not a disability; rather, the great
purpose of all our living is to learn love,
even though we must experience the pains
of love as well as the joys. To cut ourselves off from this lot of the human
would be to impoverish our lives, and
deprive ourselves of the culture of the
heart, which, if a man has not learned,
he has learned nothing. Whatever the

risks to our happiness, we cannot stand out from the lot of man, without ceasing to be men in the only true sense.

It is not easy to solve the problem of sorrow. Indeed there is no solution of it, unless the individual soul works out its own solution. Most attempts at a philosophy of sorrow just end in high-sounding words. Explanations, which profess to cover all the ground, are as futile as the ordinary blundering attempts at comfort, which only charm ache with sound and patch grief with proverbs. The sorrow of our hearts is not appreciably lessened by argument. Any kind of philosophy — any wordy explanation of the problem — is at the best poor comfort. It is not the problem which brings the pain in the first instance: it is the pain which brings the problem. The heart's bitterness is not allayed by an exposition of the doctrine of providence. Rachel who weeps for her children, the father whose little

Friendship

daughter lies dead at home, are not to
be appeased in their anguish by a nicely-
balanced system of thought.   Nor is sur-
cease of sorrow thus brought to the man
to whom has come a bereavement, or a
succession of bereavements, which makes
him feel that all the glory and joy of
life, its friendship and love and hope,
have gone down into the grave, so that
he can say,

> Three dead men have I loved,
> And thou wert last of the three.

At the same time, if it be true that
there is a meaning in friendship, a spiritual discipline to educate the heart and
train the life, it must also be true that
there is equally a meaning in the eclipse
of friendship. If we have enough faith
to see death to be good, we will find out
for ourselves why it is good. It may
teach us just what we were in danger of
forgetting, some omission in our lives,
which was making them shallow and

poor. It may be to one a sight into the mystery of sin ; to another a sight into the mystery of love. To one it comes with the lesson of patience, which is only a side of the lesson of faith ; to another it brings the message of sympathy. As we turn the subject toward the light, there come gleams of color from different facets of it.

All life is an argument for death. We cannot persist long in the effort to live the Christian life, without feeling the need for death. The higher the aims, and the truer the aspirations, the greater is the burden of living, until it would become intolerable. Sooner or later we are forced to make the confession of Job, " I would not live alway." To live forever in this sordidness, to have no reprieve from the doom of sin, no truce from the struggle of sin, would be a fearful fate.

To the Christian, therefore, death cannot be looked on as evil ; first, because it is universal, and it is universal because

128

it is God-ordained. In St. Peter's, at Rome, there are many tombs, in which death is symbolized in its traditional form as a skeleton, with the fateful hour-glass and the fearful scythe. Death is the rude reaper, who cruelly cuts off life and all the joy of life. But there is one in which death is sculptured as a sweet gentle motherly woman, who takes her wearied child home to safer and surer keeping. It is a truer thought than the other. Death is a minister of God, doing His pleasure, and doing us good.

Again, it cannot be evil because it means a fuller life, and therefore an opportunity for fuller and further service. Faith will not let a man hasten the climax; for it is in the hands of love, as he himself is. But death is the climax of life. For if all life is an argument for death, then so also all death is an argument for life.

Jowett says, in one of his letters, "I cannot sympathize in all the grounds of consolation that are sometimes offered on these melancholy occasions, but there are two things which have always seemed to me unchangeable : first, that the dead are in the hands of God, who can do for them more than we can ask or have ; and secondly, with respect to ourselves, that such losses deepen our views of life, and make us feel that we would not always be here." These are two noble grounds of consolation, and they are enough.

Death is the great argument for immortality. We cannot believe that the living, loving soul has ceased to be. We cannot believe that all those treasures of mind and heart are squandered in empty air. We will not believe it. When once we understand the meaning of the spiritual, we see the absolute certainty of eternal life ; we need no arguments for the persistence of being.

To appear for a little time and then vanish away, is the outward biography of all men, a circle of smoke that breaks, a bubble on the stream that bursts, a spark put out by a breath.

But there is another biography, a deeper and a permanent one, the biography of the soul. Everything that *appears* vanishes away : that is its fate, the fate of the everlasting hills as well as of the vapor that caps them. But that which does not appear, the spiritual and unseen, which we in our folly sometimes doubt because it does not appear, is the only reality ; it is eternal and passeth not away. The material in nature is only the garb of the spiritual, as speech is the clothing of thought. With our vulgar standards we often think of the thought as the unsubstantial and the shadowy, and the speech as the real. But speech dies upon the passing wind ; the thought alone remains. We consider the sound to be the music, whereas it is only the expression of the music, and vanishes away. Behind the material world, which waxes old as a garment, there is an eter-

nal principle, the thought of God it represents. Above the sounds there is the
music that can never die. Beneath our
lives, which vanish away, there is a vital
thing, spirit. We cannot locate it and
put our finger on it ; that is why it is permanent. The things we can put our finger on are the things which appear, and
therefore which fade and die.

So, death to the spiritual mind is only
eclipse. When there is an eclipse of the
sun it does not mean that the sun is blot-
ted out of the heavens : it only means
that there is a temporary obstruction between it and us. If we wait a little, it
passes. Love cannot die. Its forms may
change, even its objects, but its life is the
life of the universe. It is not death, but
sleep : not loss, but eclipse. The love is
only transfigured into something more
ethereal and heavenly than ever before.
Happy to have friends on earth, but hap-
pier to have friends in heaven.

And it need not be even eclipse, except

in outward form. Communion with the
unseen can mean true correspondence
with all we have loved and lost, if only
our souls were responsive. The highest
love is not starved by the absence of its
object; it rather becomes more tender
and spiritual, with more of the ideal in
it. Ordinary affection, on a lower plane,
dependent on physical attraction, or on
the earthly side of life, naturally crum-
bles to dust when its foundation is removed. But love is independent of time
or space, and as a matter of fact is puri-
fied and intensified by absence. Separation of friends is not a physical thing.
Lives can be sundered as if divided by
infinite distance, even although materially
they are near each other. This tragedy
is often enough enacted in our midst.

The converse is also true ; so that friendship does not really lose by death : it lays
up treasure in heaven, and leaves the
very earth a sacred place, made holy by
happy memories. "The ruins of Time

build mansions in Eternity," said William Blake, speaking of the death of a loved brother, with whose spirit he never ceased to converse. There are people in our homes and our streets whose highest life is with the dead. They live in another world. We can see in their eyes that their hearts are not here. It is as if they already saw the land that is very far off. It is only far off to our gross insensate senses.

The spiritual world is not outside this earth of ours. It includes it and pervades it, finding a new centre for a new circumference in every loving soul that has eyes to see the Kingdom. So, to hold commerce with the dead is not a mere figure of speech. Heaven lies about us not only in our infancy, but all our lives. We blind ourselves with dust, and in our blindness lay hold feverishly of the outside of life, mistaking the fugitive and evanescent for the truly permanent. If we only used our capacities we would

Friendship

take a more enlightened view of death. We would see it to be the entrance into a more radiant and a more abundant life not only for the friend that goes first, but for the other left behind.

Spiritual communion cannot possibly be interrupted by a physical change. It is because there is so little of the spiritual in our ordinary intercourse that death means silence and an end to communion. There is a picture of death, which, when looked at with the ordinary perspective, seems to be a hideous skull, but when seen near at hand is composed of flowers, with the eyes, in the seemingly empty sockets of the skull, formed by two fair faces of children. Death at a distance looks horrible, the ghastly spectre of the race; but with the near vision it is beautiful with youth and flowers, and when we look into its eyes we look into the stirrings of life.

Love is the only permanent relationship among men, and the permanence is

135

not an accident of it, but is of its very essence. When released from the mere magnetism of sense, instead of ceasing to exist, it only then truly comes into its largest life. If our life were more a life in the spirit, we would be sure that death can be at the worst but the eclipse of friendship. Tennyson felt this truth in his own experience, and expressed it in noble form again and again in *In Memoriam* —

> Sweet human hand and lips and eye,
> Dear heavenly friend that canst not die ;
>
> Strange friend, past, present, and to be ;
> Loved deeplier, darklier understood ;
> Behold I dream a dream of good,
> And mingle all the world with thee.
>
> Thy voice is on the rolling air ;
> I hear thee where the waters run ;
> Thou standest in the rising sun,
> And in the setting thou art fair.

It is not loss, but momentary eclipse, and the final issue is a clearer perception of immortal love, and a deeper consciousness of eternal life.

The attitude of mind, therefore, in any such bereavement — sore as the first stroke must be, since we are so much the creatures of habit, and it is hard to adjust ourselves to the new relationship — cannot be an attitude merely of resignation. That was the extent to which the imperfect revelation of the Old Testament brought men. They had to rest in their knowledge of God's faithfulness and goodness. The limit of their faith was, "The Lord gave, and the Lord hath taken away." But to resignation we can add joy. "Not dead, but sleepeth," said the Master of death and life to a sorrowing man.

For one thing it must mean the hallowing of memory. The eclipse of love makes the love fairer when the eclipse passes. The loss of the outward purifies the affection and softens the heart. It brings out into fact what was often only latent in feeling. Memory adds a tender glory to the past. We only think of the virtues of the dead : we forget their faults. This is as it should be. We rightly love the immortal part of them ; the fire has burned up the dross and left pure gold. If it is idealization, it represents that which will be, and that which really is.

We do not ask to forget ; we do not want the so-called consolations which time brings. Such an insult to the past, as forgetfulness would be, means that we have not risen to the possibilities of communion of spirit afforded us in the present. We would rather that the wound should be ever fresh than that the image of the dear past should fade. It would be a loss to our best life if it would fade. There is no sting in such a faith. Such remembrance as this, which keeps the heart green, will not cumber the life. True sentiment does not weaken, but becomes an inspiration to make our life worthy of our love. It can save even a squalid lot from sordidness; for however poor we may be in the world's goods, we are rich in happy associations in the past, and in sweet communion in the present, and in blessed hope for the future.

The Wreck of

Friendship

THEY parted — ne'er to meet again!
  But never either found another
To free the hollow heart from paining —
They stood aloof, the scars remaining,
Like cliffs which had been rent asunder,
A dreary sea now rolls between ;
But neither heat, nor frost, nor thunder,
Shall wholly do away, I ween,
The marks of that which once hath been.

COLERIDGE, *Christabel.*

The Wreck of Friendship

THE eclipse of friendship through death is not nearly so sad as the many ways in which friendship may be wrecked. There are worse losses than the losses of death; and to bury a friendship is a keener grief than to bury a friend. The latter softens the heart and sweetens the life, while the former hardens and embitters. The Persian poet Hafiz says, "Thou learnest no secret until thou knowest friendship; since to the unloving no heavenly knowledge enters." But so imperfect are our human relationships, that many a man has felt that he has bought his knowledge too dearly. Few of us go through the world without some scars on the heart, which even yet throb if the finger of memory touch them. In spite of all that has been said, and may be said in praise of this golden friendship, it has been too often found how vain is the help of man. The deepest tragedies of life have been the failure of this very relationship.

In one way or other the loss of friendship comes to all. The shores of life are strewn with wrecks. The convoy which left the harbor gaily in the sunshine cannot all expect to arrive together in the haven. There are the danger of storms and collisions, the separation of the night, and even at the best, if accidents never occur, the whole company cannot all keep up with the speed of the swiftest.

There is a certain pathos in all loss, but there is not always pain in it, or at least it is of varied quality and extent. Some losses are natural and unavoidable, quite beyond our control, the result of resistless change. Some loss is even the necessary accompaniment of gain. The loss of youth with all its possessions is

Friendship

the gain of manhood and womanhood. A
man must put away childish things, the
speech and understanding and thought of
a child. So the loss of some friendship
comes as a part of the natural course of
things, and is accepted without mutilat-
ing the life.

Many of our connections with people
are admittedly casual and temporary.
They exist for mutual convenience
through common interest at the time, or
common purpose, or common business.
None of the partners asks for more than
the advantage each derives from the connection. When it comes to an end, we
let slip the cable easily, and say good-bye
with a cheery wave. With many people
we meet and part in all friendliness and
good feeling, and will be glad to meet
again, but the parting does not tear our
affections by the roots. When the business is transacted the tie is loosed, and
we each go our separate ways without
much regret.

10   145

At other times there is no thought of gain, except the mutual advantage of conversation or companionship. We are pleasant to each other, and enjoy the intercourse of kindred tastes. Most of us have some pleasant recollections of happy meetings with interesting people, perhaps on holiday times, when we felt we would be glad to see them again if fortune turned round the wheel again to the same place; but, though hardly ever did it come about that an opportunity of meeting has occurred, we do not feel that our life is much the poorer for the loss.

Also, we *grow* out of some of our friendships. This is to be expected, since so many of them are formed thoughtlessly, or before we really knew either ourselves or our friends. They never meant very much to us. Most boyish friendships as a rule do not last long, because they are not based on the qualities which wear well. Schoolboy comradeships are usually due to propinquity rather than to character. They are the fruit of accident rather than of affinity of soul. Boys grow out of these as they grow out of their clothes. Now and again they suffer from growing pains, but it is more discomfort than anything else.

It is sad to look back and realize how few of one's early companionships remain, but it is not possible to blame either party for the loss. Distance, separation of interest, difference of work, all operate to divide. When athletics seemed the end of existence, friendship was based on football and baseball. But as life opens out, other standards are set up, and a new principle of selection takes its place. When the world is seen to be more than a ball-ground, when it is recognized to be a stage on which men play many parts, a new sort of intimacy is demanded, and it does not follow that it will be with the same persons. Such loss as this is the condition which accompanies the gain of growth.

There is more chance for the permanence of friendships formed a little later.
It must not be too long after this period,
however; for, when the generous time of
youth has wholly passed, it becomes hard
to make new connections.   Men get over-
burdened with cares and personal con-
cerns, and grow cautious about making
advances.   In youth the heart is responsive and ready to be generous, and the
hand aches for the grasp of a comrade's
hand, and the mind demands fellowship
in the great thoughts that are beginning
to dawn upon it.   The closest friendships
are formed early in life, just because then
we are less cautious, more open to impressions, and readier to welcome self-revela-
tions.   After middle life a man does not
find it easy to give himself away, and
keeps a firmer hand on his feelings.
Whatever are the faults of youth, it is
unworldly in its estimates as a rule, and
uncalculating in its thoughts of the
future.

Friendship

The danger to such friendship is the danger of just letting it lapse. As life spreads out before the eager feet, new interests crop up, new relations are formed, and the old tie gets worn away, from want of adding fresh strands to it. We may believe the advice about not forsaking an old friend because the new is not comparable to him, but we can neglect it by merely letting things slip past, which if used would be a new bond of union.

As it is easier for some temperaments to make friends, it is easier for some dispositions to keep them. Little faults of manner, little occasions of thoughtlessness, or lack of the little courtesies, do more to separate people than glaring mistakes. There are some men so built that it is difficult to remain on very close terms with them, there are so many corners to knock against. Even strength of character, if unmodified by sweetness of disposition, adds to the difficulty

of pulling together. Strong will can so
easily develop into self-will ; decision can
become dogmatism ; wit, the salt of conversation, loses its savor when it becomes
ill-natured ; a faculty for argument is in
danger of being mere quarrelsomeness.

The ordinary amenities of life must be
preserved among friends. We can never
feel very safe with the man whose hu-
mor tends to bitter speaking or keen sar-
casm, or with the man who flares up
into hasty speech at every or no provo-
cation, or with the man who is argu-
mentative and assertive, —

> Who 'd rather on a gibbet dangle
> Than miss his dear delight to wrangle.

There are more breaches of the peace
among friends through sins of speech,
than from any other cause. We do not
treat our friends with enough respect.
We make the vulgar mistake of looking
upon the common as if it were therefore cheap in nature. We ought rather

to treat our friend with a sort of sacred familiarity, as if we appreciated the precious gift his friendship is.

Every change in a man's life brings a risk of letting go something of the past, which it is a loss to part with. A change of work, or a change of residence, or entrance into a larger sphere, brings a certain engrossment which leads to neglect of the richest intercourse in the past life. To many a man, even marriage has had a drop of bitterness in it, because it has somehow meant the severing of old and sacred links. This may be due to the vulgar reason of wives' quarrels, the result of petty jealousy; but it may be due also to pre-occupation and a subtle form of selfishness. The fire needs to be kept alivè with fuel. To preserve it, there must be forethought, and care, and love expended as before.

Friendship may lapse through the *misfortune of distance.* Absence does not

always make the heart grow fonder. It
only does so, when the heart is securely
fixed, and when it is a heart worth fix-
ing. More often the other proverb is
truer, that it is out of sight out of mind.
It is so easy for a man to become self-
centred, and to impoverish his affections
through sheer neglect. Ties once close
get frayed and strained till they break,
and we discover that we have said fare-
well to the past. Some kind of intercourse is needed to maintain friendship.
There is a pathos about this gradual
drifting away of lives, borne from each
other, it sometimes seems, by opposing
tides, as if a resistless power separated
them,

> And bade betwixt their souls to be
> The unplumbed, salt, estranging sea.

Or friendship may lapse through the
fault of silence. The misfortune of distance may be overcome by love, but the
fault of silence crushes out feeling as the

Friendship

falling rain kills the kindling beacon.
Even the estrangements and misunderstandings which will arise to all could
not long remain, where there is a frank
and candid interchange of thought.
Hearts grow cold toward each other
through neglect. There is a suggestive
word from the old Scandinavian *Edda*,
"Go often to the house of thy friend;
for weeds soon choke up the unused
path." It is hard to overcome again the
alienation caused by neglect; for there
grows up a sense of resentment and injured feeling.

Among the petty things which wreck
friendships, none is so common and so
unworthy as money. It is pitiable that
it should be so. Thackeray speaks of the
remarkable way in which a five-pound
note will break up a half-century's attachment between two brethren, and it
is a common cynical remark of the world
that the way to lose a friend is to lend
him money. There is nothing which

seems to affect the mind more, and color
the very heart's blood, than money.
There seems a curse in it sometimes, so
potent is it for mischief. Poverty, if it
be too oppressive grinding down the face,
may often hurt the heart-life; but perhaps oftener still it only reveals what
true treasures there are in the wealth of
the affections. Whereas, we know what
heartburnings, and rivalries, and envy-
ings, are occasioned by this golden apple
of discord. Most of the disputes which
separate brethren are about the dividing
of the inheritance, and it does seem to be
the case that few friendships can survive
the test of money.

> Neither a borrower, nor a lender be ;
> For loan oft loses both itself and friend.

There must be something wrong with
the friendship which so breaks down. It
ought to be able to stand a severer strain
than that. But the inner reason of the
failure is often that there has been a

moral degeneracy going on, and a weakening of the fibre of character on one side, or on both sides. The particular dispute, whether it be about money or about anything else, is only the occasion which reveals the slackening of the morale. The innate delicacy and self-respect of the friend who asks the favor may have been damaged through a series of similar importunities, or there may have been a growing hardness of heart and selfishness in the friend who refuses the request. Otherwise, if two are on terms of communion, it is hard to see why the giving or receiving of this service should be any more unworthy than any other help, which friends can grant to each other. True commerce of the heart should make all other needful commerce possible. Communion includes communism. To have things in common does not seem difficult, when there is love in common.

Friendship has also been wrecked by

outside means, by the evil of others,
through the evil speaking, or the envy,
or the whispering tongues that delight in
scandal. Some mean natures rejoice in
sowing discord, carrying tales with just
the slightest turn of a phrase, or even a
tone of the voice, which gives a sinister
reading to an innocent word or act.
Frankness can always prevent such from
permanently wrecking friendship. Besides, we should judge no man, still less
a trusted friend, by a report of an incident or a hasty word. We should judge
our friend by his record, by what we
know of his character. When anything
inconsistent with that character comes
before our notice, it is only justice to him
to at least suspend judgment, and it
would be wisdom to refuse to credit it at
all.

We sometimes wonder to find a friend
cold and distant to us, and perhaps we
moralize on the fickleness and inconstancy of men, but the reason may be

Friendship

to seek in ourselves. We cannot expect the pleasure of friendship without the duty, the privilege without the responsibility. We cannot break off the threads of the web, and then, when the mood is on us, continue it as though nothing had happened. If such a breakage has occurred, we must go back and patiently join the threads together again. Thoughtlessness has done more harm in this respect than ill-will. If we have lost a friend through selfish neglect, the loss is ours, and we cannot expect to take up the story where we left off years ago. There is a serene impudence about the treatment some mete out to their friends, dropping them whenever it suits, and thinking to take them up when it happens once more to suit. We cannot expect to walk with another, when we have gone for miles along another way. We will have to go back, and catch him up again. If the fault has been ours, desire and shame will give our feet wings.

The real source of separation is ultimately a spiritual one. We cannot walk with another unless we are agreed. The lapse of friendship is often due to this, that one has let the other travel on alone. If one has sought pleasure, and the other has sought truth; if one has cumbered his life with the trivial and the petty, and the other has filled his with high thoughts and noble aspirations; if their hearts are on different levels, it is natural that they should now be apart. We cannot stay behind with the camp-followers, and at the same time fight in the van with the heroes. If we would keep our best friends, we must go with them in sympathy, and be able to share their thoughts. In the letters of Dean Stanley, there is one from Jowett to Stanley, which brings out this necessity. "I earnestly hope that the friendship, which commenced between us many years ago, may be a blessing to last us through life. I feel that if it is to be so we must both go onward, otherwise the tear and wear of life, and the 'having travelled over each other's minds,' and a thousand accidents will be sufficient to break it off. I have often felt the inability to converse with you, but never for an instant the least alienation. There is no one who would not think me happy in having such a friend."

It is not, however, so much the equal pace of the mind which is necessary, as the equal pace of the spirit. We may think about a very brilliant friend that he will outstrip us, and outgrow us. The fear is natural, but if there be spiritual oneness it is an unfounded fear.

> Yet oft, when sundown skirts the moor,
> An inner trouble I behold,
> A spectral doubt which makes me cold,
> That I should be thy mate no more.

But love is not dependent on intellect. The great bond of union is not that both parties are alike in mind, but that they are akin in soul. Mere intellect only divides men further than the ordinary natural and artificial distinctions that already exist. There are endless instances of this disuniting influence to be seen, in the contempt of learning for ignorance, the derisive attitude which knowledge assumes toward simplicity, the metropolitan disdain for provincial Galilee, the *rabies theologica* which is ever ready to declare that this people that knoweth not the law is accursed. It is love, not logic, which can unite men. Love is the one solvent to break down all barriers, and love has other grounds for its existence than merely intellectual ones. So that although similarity of taste is another bond and is perhaps necessary for the perfect friendship, it is not its foundation; and if the foundation be not undermined, there is no reason why difference of mental power should wreck the structure.

However it happen that friends are separated, it is always sad; for the loss of a friendship is the loss of an ideal.

Friendship

Sadder than the pathos of unmated hearts
is the pathos of severed souls. It is always a pain to find a friend look on us
with cold stranger's eyes, and to know
ourselves dead of hopes of future intimacy. It is a pain even when we have
nothing to blame ourselves with, much
more so when we feel that ours is the
fault. It would not seem to matter very
much, if it were not such a loss to both;
for friendship is one of the appointed
means of saving the life from worldli-
ness and selfishness. It is the greatest
education in the world; for it is education of the whole man, of the affections
as well as the intellect. Nothing of
worldly success can make up for the
want of it. And true friendship is also
a moral preservative. It teaches something of the joy of service, and the
beauty of sacrifice. We cannot live an
utterly useless life, if we have to think
for, and act for, another. It keeps love
in the heart, and keeps God in the life.

The Wreck of

The greatest and most irretrievable wreck of friendship is the result of a moral breakdown in one of the associates. Worse than the separation of the grave is the desolation of the heart by faithlessness. More impassable than the gulf of distance with the estranging sea, more separating than the gulf of death, is the great gulf fixed between souls through deceit and shame. It is as the sin of Judas. Said a sorrowful Psalmist, who had known this experience, "Mine own familiar friend in whom I trusted, which did eat of my bread, hath lifted up his heel against me." And another Psalmist sobs out the same lament, "It was not an enemy that reproached me, then I could have borne it, but it was thou, a man mine equal, my guide and mine acquaintance. We took sweet counsel together, and walked into the house of God in company." The loss of a friend by any of the common means is not so hard, as to find a friend faithless.

Friendship

The trustful soul has often been disillusioned thus. The rod has broken in the hand that leaned on it, and has left its red wound on the palm. There is a deeper wound on the heart.

The result of such a breakdown of comradeship is often bitterness, and cynical distrust of man. It is this experience which gives point to the worldling's sneer, Defend me from my friends, I can defend myself from my enemies. We cannot wonder sometimes at the cynicism. It is like treason within the camp, against which no man can guard. It is a stab in the back, a cowardly assassination of the heart. Treachery like this usually means a sudden fall from the ideal for the deceived one, and the ideal can only be recovered, if at all, by a slow and toilsome ascent, foot by foot and step by step.

Failure of one often leads to distrust of all. This is the terrible responsibility of friendship. We have more than the happiness of our friend in our power; we have his faith. Most men who are cynical about women are so, because of the inconstancy of one. Most sneers at friendship are, to begin with at least, the expression of individual pain, because the man has known the shock of the lifted heel. Distrust works havoc on the character; for it ends in unbelief of goodness itself. And distrust always meets with its own likeness, and is paid back in its own coin. Suspicion breeds suspicion, and the conduct of life on such principles becomes a tug-of-war in which Greek is matched with Greek.

The social virtues, which keep the whole community together, are thus closely allied to the supreme virtue of friendship. Aristotle had reason in making it the *nexus* between his Ethics and his Politics. Truth, good faith, honest dealing between man and man, are necessary for any kind of intercourse, even that of business. Men can do nothing with each other, if they have not a certain minimum

Friendship

of trust. There have been times when there seems to be almost an epidemic of faithlessness, when the social bond seems loosened, when men's hands are raised against each other, when confidence is paralyzed, and people hardly know whom to trust.

The prophet Micah, who lived in such a time, expresses this state of distrust: "Trust ye not any friend, put ye no confidence in a familiar friend. A man's enemies are of his own household." This means anarchy, and society becomes like a bundle of sticks with the cord cut. The cause is always a decay of religion; for law is based on morality, and morality finds its strongest sanction in religion. Selfishness results in anarchy, a reversion to the Ishmaelite type of life.

The story of the French Revolution has in it some of the darkest pages in the history of modern civilization, due to the breakdown of social trust. The Revolution, like Saturn, took to devouring her own children. Suspicion, during the reign of terror, brooded over the heads of men, and oppressed their hearts. The ties of blood and fellowship seemed broken, and the sad words of Christ had their horrid fulfilment, that the brother would deliver up the brother to death, and the father the child, and the children rise up against the parents and cause them to be put to death. There are some awful possibilities in human nature. In Paris of these days a man had to be ever on his guard, to watch his acts, his words, even his looks. It meant for a time a collapse of the whole idea of the state. It was a panic, worse than avowed civil war. Friendship, of course, could have little place in such a frightful palsy of mutual confidence, though there were, for the honor of the race, some noble exceptions. The wreck of friendship through deceit is always a step toward social anarchy; for it helps to break down trust and good faith among men.

Friendship

The wreck of friendship is also a blow
to religion. Many have lost their faith
in God, because they have lost, through
faithlessness, their faith in man. Doubt
of the reality of love becomes doubt of
the reality of the spiritual life. To be
unable to see the divine in man, is to
have the eyes blinded to the divine anywhere. Deception in the sphere of love
shakes the foundation of religion. Its result is atheism, not perhaps as a conscious
speculative system of thought, but as a
subtle practical influence on conduct. It
corrupts the fountain of life, and taints
the whole stream. Despair of love, if
final and complete, would be despair of
God; for God is love. Thus, the wreck
of friendship often means a temporary
wreck of faith. It ought not to be so;
but that there is a danger of it should
impress us with a deeper sense of the
responsibility attached to our friendships.
Our life follows the fortunes of our love.

The Renewing of
Friendship

PERHAPS we may go further, and say that friends, whose friendship has been broken off, should not entirely forget their former intercourse; and that just as we hold that we ought to serve friends before strangers, so former friends have some claims upon us on the ground of past friendship, unless extraordinary depravity were the cause of our parting. — ARISTOTLE.

The Renewing of Friendship

IT is a sentiment of the poets and romancers that love is rather helped by quarrels. There must be some truth in it, as we find the idea expressed a hundred times in different forms in literature. We find it among the wisdom of the ancients, and it remains still as one of the conventional properties of the dramatist, and one of the accepted traditions of the novelist. It is expressed in maxim and apothegm, in play and poem. One of our old pre-Elizabethan writers has put it in classic form in English : —

The falling out of faithful friends is the renewing of love.

It is the chief stock-in-trade of the writer of fiction, to depict the misunderstandings which arise between two per-

171

sons, through the sin of one, or the folly
of both, or the villainy of a third ; then
comes the means by which the tangled
skein is unravelled, and in the end everything is satisfactorily explained, and the
sorely-tried characters are ushered into a
happiness stronger and sweeter than ever
before.   Friends quarrel, and are miser-
able in their state of separation ; and
afterward, when the friendship is renewed, it is discovered that the bitter
dispute was only a blessing in disguise, as
the renewal itself was an exquisite pleasure, and the result has been a firmer and
more stable relationship of love and trust.

The truth in this sentiment is, of course,
the evident one, that a man often only
wakens to the value of a possession when
he is in danger of losing it.   The force of
a current is sometimes only noted when
it is opposed by an obstacle.   Two persons may discover, by a temporary alienation, how much they really care for
each other.   It may be that previously

Friendship

they took things for granted. Their affection had lost its first glitter, and was accepted as a commonplace. Through some misunderstanding or dispute, they broke off their friendly relationship, feeling sure that they had come to an end of their regard. They could never again be on the same close terms; hot words had been spoken; taunts and reproaches had passed; eyes had flashed fire, and they parted in anger — only to learn that their love for each other was as real and as strong as ever. The very difference revealed the true union of hearts that had existed. They had been blind to the strength of their mutual regard, till it was so painfully brought to their notice. The love is renewed with a more tender sense of its sacredness, and a more profound feeling of its strength. The dissensions only displayed the union; the discord drove them to a fuller harmony. This is a natural and common experience.

173

But a mistake may easily be made by confusing cause and effect. "The course of true love never did run smooth" — but the obstacles in the channel do not *produce* the swiftness and the volume of the stream ; they only *show* them. There may be an unsuspected depth and force for the first time brought to light when the stream strikes a barrier, but the barrier is merely the occasion, not the cause, of the revelation. To mistake the one for the other, may lead to a false and stupid policy. Many, through this mistake, act as though dissension were of the very nature of affection, and as if the one must necessarily react on the other for good. Some foolish people will sometimes even produce disagreement for the supposed pleasure of agreeing once more, and quarrel for the sake of making it up again.

Rather, the end of love is near at hand, when wrangling can live in its presence. It is not true that love is helped by quarrels, except in the small sense already indicated. A man may quarrel once too often with his friend, and a brother offended, says the proverb, is harder to be won than a strong city, and such contentions are like the bars of a castle. It is always a dangerous experiment to wilfully test affection, besides being often a cruel one. Disputing is a shock to confidence, and without confidence friendship cannot continue. A state of feud, even though a temporary one, often embitters the life, and leaves its mark on the heart. Desolated homes and lonely lives are witnesses of the folly of any such policy. From the root of bitterness there cannot possibly blossom any of the fair flowers of love. The surface truth of the poets' sentiment we have acknowledged and accounted for, but it is only a surface truth. The best of friends will fall out, and the best of them will renew their friendship, but it is always at a great risk, and sometimes it strains the

foundations of their esteem for each
other to shaking :

> And blessings on the falling out
> That all the more endears,
> When we fall out with those we love
> And kiss again with tears !

But in any serious rupture of friendship
it can only be a blessing when it means
the tears of repentance, and these are
often tears of blood. In all renewing
there must be an element of repentance,
and however great the joy of having
regained the old footing, there is the
memory of pain, and the presence of
regret. To cultivate contention as an
art, and to trade upon the supposed benefit of renewing friendship, is a folly which
brings its own retribution.

The disputatious person for this reason
never makes a good friend. In friendship
men look for peace, and concord, and some
measure of content. There are enough
battles to fight outside, enough jarring

and jostling in the street, enough disputing in the market-place, enough discord in
the workaday world, without having to
look for contention in the realm of the
inner life also. There, if anywhere, we
ask for an end of strife. Friendship is the
sanctuary of the heart, and the peace of
the sanctuary should brood over it. Its
chiefest glory is that the dust and noise
of contest are excluded.

It must needs be that offences come.
It is not only that the world is full of
conflict and controversy, and every man
must take his share in the fights of his
time. We are born into the battle; we
are born for the battle. But apart from
the outside strife, from which we cannot separate ourselves, and do not desire
to separate ourselves if we are true men,
the strange thing is that it looks as if it
must needs be that offences come even
among brethren. The bitterest disputes
in life are among those who are nearest
each other in spirit. We do not quarrel

with the man in the street, the man with
whom we have little or no communication. He has not the chance, nor the
power, to chafe our soul, and ruffle our
temper. If need be, we can afford to
despise, or at least to neglect him. It is
the man of our own household, near us
in life and spirit, who runs the risk of
the only serious dissensions with us. The
man with whom we have most points
of contact presents the greatest number
of places where difference can occur. Only
from circles that touch each other can
a tangent strike off from the same point.
A man can only make enemies among
his friends. A certain amount of oppo-
sition and enmity a man must be prepared for in this world, unless he live
a very invertebrate life. Outside opposi-
tion cannot embitter, for it cannot touch
the soul. But that two who have walked
as friends, one in aim and one in heart,
perhaps of the same household of faith,
should stand face to face with hard brows

178

and gleaming eyes, should speak as foes and not as lovers of the same love, is, in spite of the poets and romancers, the bitterest moment of life.

There are some we cannot hurt even if we would ; whom all the venom of our nature could not touch, because we mean nothing to them. But there are others in our power, whom we can stab with a word, and these are our brethren, our familiar friends, our comrades at work, our close associates, our fellow laborers in God's vineyard. It is not the crowd that idly jostle us in the street who can hurt us to the quick, but a familiar friend in whom we trusted. He has a means of ingress barred to strangers, and can strike home as no other can. This explains why family quarrels, ruptures in the inner circle, Church disputes, are so bitter. They come so near us. An offended brother is hard to win, because the very closeness of the previous intimacy brings a rankling sense of injustice and the resentment of injured love. An injury from the hand of a friend seems such a wanton thing, and the heart hardens itself with the sense of wrong, and a separation ensues like the bars of a castle.

It must needs be that offences come, but woe unto him by whom they come. The strife-makers find in themselves, in their barren heart and empty life, their own appropriate curse. The blow they strike comes back upon themselves. Worse than the choleric temperament is the peevish, sullen nature. The one usually finds a speedy repentance for his hot and hasty mood; the other is a constant menace to friendship, and acts like a perpetual irritant. Its root is selfishness, and it grows by what it feeds on.

When offences do come, we may indeed use them as opportunities for growth in gracious ways, and thus turn them into blessings on the lives of both. To the offended it may be an occasion for pa-

Friendship

tience and forgiveness ; to the offender,
an occasion for humility and frank confession ; and to both, a renewing of love
less open to offence in the future.   There
are some general counsels about the making up of differences, though each case
needs special treatment for itself, which
will easily be found if once the desire for
concord be established.   Christ's recipe
for a quarrel among brethren is : " If thy
brother shall trespass against thee, go and
tell him his fault between thee and him
alone ; if he shall hear thee, thou hast
gained thy brother."

Much of our dissension is due to misunderstanding, which could be put right
by a few honest words and a little open
dealing.   Human beings so often live at
cross purposes with each other, when a
frank word, or a simple confession of
wrong, almost a look or a gesture, would
heal the division.   Resentment grows
through brooding over a fancied slight.
Hearts harden themselves in silence, and,

as time goes on, it becomes more difficult to break through the silence. Often there are strained relations among men, who, at the bottom of their hearts, have sincere respect for each other, and smouldering affection also, which only needs a little coaxing of the spark to burst out again into a dancing flame. There is a terrible waste of human friendship, a waste of power which might be used to bless all our lives, through our sinful separations, our selfish exclusiveness, our resentful pride. We let the sweetest souls we have met die without acknowledging our debt to them. We stand aside in haughty isolation, till the open grave opens our sealed hearts — too late. We let the chance of reconciliation pass till it is irrevocable. Most can remember a tender spot in the past somewhere, a sore place, a time when discord entered with another they loved, and

> Each spake words of high disdain
> And insult to his heart's best brother.

Friendship

And in some cases, as with the friends in Coleridge's great poem, the parting has been eternal, and neither has ever since found another such friend to fill the life with comfort, and free the hollow heart from paining.

There is more evil from such a state of discord than the mere loss it is to both; it influences the whole heart-life, creating sometimes bitterness, sometimes universal suspicion, sometimes cynicism. Hatred is contagious, as love is. They have an effect on the whole character, and are not confined to the single incident which causes the love or the hate. To hate a single one of God's creatures is to harden the heart to some extent against all. Love is the centre of a circle, which broadens out in ever-widening circumference. Dante tells us in *La Vita Nuova* that the effect of his love for Beatrice was to open his heart to all, and to sweeten all his life. He speaks of the surpassing virtue of her very salutation to him in the street. "When she appeared in any place, it seemed to me, by the hope of her excellent salutation, that there was no man mine enemy any longer; and such warmth of charity came upon me that most certainly in that moment I would have pardoned whomsoever had done me an injury; and if any one should then have questioned me concerning any matter, I could only have said unto him ' Love,' with a countenance clothed in humbleness." His love bred sweetness in his mind, and took in everything within the blessed sweep of its range. Hatred also is the centre of a circle, which has a baneful effect on the whole life. We cannot have bitterness or resentment in our mind without its coloring every thought and affection. Hate of one will affect our attitude toward all.

If, then, we possess the spirit to be reconciled with an offended or an offending brother, there are some things which may be said about the tactics of renewing the broken tie. There is needed a certain tactful considerateness. In all such questions the grace of the act depends as much on the *manner* of it, as on the act itself. The grace of the fairest act may be hurt by a boorish blemish of manner. Many a graceful act is spoiled by a graceless touch, as a generous deed can be ruined by a grudging manner. An air of condescension will destroy the value of the finest charity. There is a forgiveness which is no forgiveness — formal, constrained, from the teeth and lips outward. It does not come as the warm breath which has had contact with the blood of the heart. The highest forgiveness is so full and free, that it is forgetfulness. It is complete as the forgiveness of God.

If there is something in the method of the approach, there is perhaps more in the time of it. It ought to be chosen carefully and considerately ; for it may be

135

that the other has not been prepared for
the renewal by thought and feeling, as
the man who makes the advances has
been. No hard and fast rule can be for-
mulated when dealing with such a com-
plex and varied subject as man. So much
depends on temper and character. One
man taken by surprise reveals his true
feeling; another, when taken off his
guard, is irritated, and shuts up his heart
in a sort of instinctive self-defence. The
thoughtfulness of love will suggest the
appropriate means, but some emphasis
may rightly be given to the phrase in
Christ's counsel, " between thee and him
alone." Let there be an opportunity for
a frank and private conversation. To
appeal to an estranged friend before witnesses induces to special pleading, making
the witnesses the jury, asking for a ver-
dict on either side ; and the result is that
both are still convinced they have right
on their side, and that they have been
wronged.

Friendship

If the fault of the estrangement lies with us, the burden of confession should rest upon us also. To go to him with sincere penitence is no more than our duty. Whether the result be successful or not, it will mean a blessing for our own soul. Humility brings its own reward; for it brings God into the life. Even if we have cause to suspect that the offended brother will not receive us kindly, still such reparation as we can make is at least the gate to reconciliation. It may be too late, but confession will lighten the burden on our own heart. Our brother may be so offended that he is harder to be won than a strong city, but he is far more worth winning; and even if the effort be unsuccessful, it is better than the cowardice which suffers a bloodless defeat.

If, on the other hand, the fault was not ours, our duty is still clear. It should be even easier to take the initiative in such a case; for after all it is much easier to forgive than to submit to be forgiven. To

187

some natures it is hard to be laid under
an obligation, and the generosity of love
must be shown by the offended brother.
He must show the other his fault gently
and generously, not parading his forgiveness like a virtue, but as if the favor were
on his side — as it is. Christ made forgiveness the test of spirituality. If we do
not know the grace of forgiveness, we
do not know how gracious life may be.
The highest happiness is not a matter of
possessions and material gains, but has
its source in a heart at peace; and thus
it is that the renewing of friendship has a
spiritual result. If we are revengeful,
censorious, judging others harshly, always
putting the worst construction on a word
or an act, uncharitable, unforgiving, we
certainly cannot claim kinship with the
spirit of the Lord Jesus. St. Paul made
the opposite the very test of the spiritual
man : " Brethren, if a man be overtaken
in a fault, ye which are spiritual restore
such an one in the spirit of meekness."

Friendship

If we knew all, we would forgive all.
If we knew all the facts, the things
which produced the petulance, the sore-
ness which caused the irritation, we
would be ready to pardon; for we
would understand the temptation. If
we knew all, our hearts would be full of
pitiful love even for those who have
wronged us. They have wronged themselves more than they can possibly wrong
us; they have wounded a man to their
own hurt. To think kindly once more
of a separated friend, to soften the heart
toward an offending brother, will bring
the blessing of the Peace-maker, the blessing of the Reconciler. The way to be
sure of acting this part is to pray for him.
We cannot remain angry with another,
when we pray for him. Offence departs,
when prayer comes. The captivity of
Job was turned, when he prayed for his
friends.

If we stubbornly refuse the renewing
of friendship, it is an offence against re-

ligion also. Only love can fulfil the law of Christ. His is the Gospel of reconciliation, and the greater reconciliation includes the lesser. The friends of Christ must be friends of one another. That ought to be accepted as an axiom. To be reconciled to God carries with it at least a disposition of heart, which makes it easy to be reconciled to men also. We have cause to suspect our religion, if it does not make us gentle, and forbearing, and forgiving; if the love of our Lord does not so flood our hearts as to cleanse them of all bitterness, and spite, and wrath. If a man is nursing anger, if he is letting his mind become a nest of foul passions, malice, and hatred, and evil wishing, how dwelleth the love of God in him?

If we cannot, at need, even humiliate ourselves to win our brother, it is difficult to see where our religion comes in, especially when we think what humiliation Christ suffered, that He might recon-

Friendship

cile us to God, and make us friends again
with our heavenly Father, and renew our
broken love. Whatever be our faith and
works, and however correct be our creed
and conduct, if we are giving place to
anger, if we are stiffening ourselves in
strife and disdain, we are none of His,
who was meek and lowly of heart. We
may come to the Sanctuary with lips full
of praises and eyes full of prayers, with
devotion in our hearts and gifts in our
hand, but God will spurn our worship
and despise our gifts. It is not a small
matter, this renewing of friendship, but
is the root of religion itself, and is well
made the very test of spiritual-minded-
ness. "If thou bring thy gift to the
altar, and there rememberest that thy
brother hath aught against thee, leave
there thy gift before the altar, and
go thy way; first be reconciled to thy
brother, and then come and offer thy
gift." Misunderstandings and estrangements will arise, occasions will come when

it seems as if not even love and forbearance can avoid a quarrel, but surely Christ has died in vain if His grace cannot save us from the continuance of strife.

Such renewing of love, done with this high motive, will indeed bring an added joy, as the poets have declared. The very pain will give zest to the pleasure. We will take the great gift of friendship with a new sense of its beauty and sacredness. We will walk more softly because of the experience, and more than ever will tremble lest we lose it. For days after the reconciliation, we will go about with the feeling that the benediction of the peace-makers rests on our head and clings round our feet.

But more than any personal joy from the renewed friendship, we will have the smile of God on our life. We will know that we have done what is well pleasing in His sight. Sweeter than the peace which comes from being at one with men,

Friendship

is the peace which comes from being at
one with God.   It settles on the soul
like the mist on the mountains, envelop-
ing and enswathing it.   It comes to our
fevered life as a great calm.   Over the
broken waters there hovers the golden
glory of God's eternal peace.

And more even than all that, we will
have gained a new insight into the love
of the Father, and into the sacrifice of
the Son.   We will understand a little
more of the mystery of the Love which
became poor, which gladly went into the
wilderness to seek and to save the lost.
The cross will gain new and rich significance to us, and all the world will be an
arena in which is enacted the spectacle of
God's great love.   The world is bathed
in the love of God, as it is flooded by
the blessed sun.   If we are in the light
and walk in love, our walk will be with
God, and His gentleness will make us
great.   There is intended an ever fuller
education in the meaning, and in the life

13   193

of love, until the assurance reaches us that nothing can separate us from love. Even death, which sunders us from our friends, cannot permanently divide us. In the great Home-coming and Reunion of hearts, all the veils which obscure feeling will be torn down, and we shall know each other better, and shall love each other better.

But every opportunity carries a penalty; every privilege brings with it a warning. If we will not live the life of love, if we harden our heart against a brother offended, we will find in our need even the great and infinite love of God shut against us, harder to be won than a strong city, ribbed and stockaded as the bars of a castle. To the unforgiving there is no forgiveness. To the hard, and relentless, and loveless, there is no love. To the selfish, there is no heaven.

The Limits of
Friendship

IF thy brother, the son of thy mother, or thy son, or thy daughter, or the wife of thy bosom, or thy friend which is as thine own soul, entice thee secretly, saying, Let us go and serve other gods, thou shalt not consent unto him, nor hearken unto him, but thine hand shall be first upon him to put him to death, and afterward the hand of all the people; because he hath sought to thrust thee away from the Lord thy God.

DEUTERONOMY.

Yet each will have one anguish — his own soul,
Which perishes of cold.

MATTHEW ARNOLD.

The Limits of Friendship

FRIENDSHIP, at its very best and
purest, has limits. At its beginning, it seems to have no conditions, and to be capable of endless
development. In the first flush of new-
born love it seems almost an insult to
question its absolute power to meet every
demand made upon it. The exquisite
joy of understanding, and being understood, is too keen to let us believe, that
there may be a terminal line, beyond
which we may not pass. Friendship
comes as a mystery, formless, undefined,
without set bounds; and it is often a sore
experience to discover that it is circum-
scribed, and limited like everything human. At first to speak of it as having
qualifications was a profanation, and to
find them out came as a disillusionment.

Yet the discovery is not all a loss. The limitless is also the vague, and it is well to know the exact terms implied in a relationship. Of course we learn through experience the restrictions on all intimacy, and if we are wise we learn to keep well within the margin ; but many a disappointment might have been saved, if we had understood the inherent limitations of the subject. These are the result of personality. Each partner is after all a distinct individual, with will, and conscience, and life apart, with a personal responsibility which none can take from him, and with an individual bias of mind and heart which can never be left out of account.

As is to be expected, some of the limits of friendship are not essential to the relation, but are due to a *defect* in the relation, perhaps an idiosyncrasy of character or a peculiarity of temper. Some of the limits are self-imposed, and arise from mistake of folly. A friend may be too exacting, and may make excessive

198

demands, which strain the bond to the breaking point. There is often a good deal of selfishness in the affection, which asks for absorption, and is jealous of other interests. Jealousy is usually the fruit, not of love, but of self-love. Life is bigger than any relationship, and covers more ground. The circles of life may intersect, and part of each be common to the other, but there will be an area on both sides exclusive to each; and even if it were possible for the circles to be concentric, it could hardly be that the circumference of the two could be the same; one would be, almost without a doubt, of larger radius than the other. It is not identity which is the aim and the glory of friendship, but unity in the midst of difference. To strive at identity is to be certain of failure, and it deserves failure; for it is the outcome of selfishness. A man's friend is not his property, to be claimed as his exclusive possession. Jealousy is an ignoble vice, because it has its roots in egotism. It also destroys affection, since it is an evidence of want of trust, and trust is essential to friendship.

There are physical limits to friendship, if nothing else. There are material barriers to be surmounted, before human beings really get into touch with each other, even in the slightest degree. The bodily organs, through which alone we can enter into communication, carry with them their own disabilities. The senses are at the best limited in their range, and are ever exposed to error. Flesh stands in the way of a complete revelation of soul. Human feet cannot enter past the threshold of the soul's abode. The very means of self-revelation is a self-concealment. The medium, by which alone we know, darkens, if it does not distort, the object. Words obscure thought, by the very process through which alone thought is possible for us ; and the fleshly wrappings of the soul hide it, at the same time that they make it visible.

Friendship

And if there are physical limits to friendship, there are greater mental limits. The needs of living press on us, and drive us into different currents of action. Our varied experience colors all our thought, and gives a special bias to our mind. There is a personal equation which must always be taken into account. This is the charm of intercourse, but it is also a limitation. We do not travel over the same ground; we meet, but we also part. However great the sympathy, it is not possible completely to enter into another man's mind, and look at a subject with his eyes. Much of our impatience with each other, and most of our misunderstandings, are caused by this natural limitation. The lines along which our minds travel can at the best be asymptotic, approaching each other indefinitely near, but never quite coinciding.

The greatest limit of friendship, of which these other are but indications, is the spiritual fact of the separate person-

ality of each human being. This is seen
most absolutely in the sphere of morals.
The ultimate standard for a man is his
own individual conscience, and neither
the constraint of affection, nor the authority of numbers, can atone for false-
ness there. One of the most forceful
illustrations of this final position of all
religion is to be found in the passage of
terrific intensity from the Book of Deuteronomy, which we have transcribed as
a preface to this chapter. The form of
the passage of course gets its coloring
from the needs of the time and the temper of the age. The Book of Deuteronomy is so sure that the law of God is
necessary for the life of Israel, and that
departure from it will mean national
ruin, that it will shrink from nothing
needed to preserve the truth. Its warnings against being led away to idolatry
are very instant and solemn. Every pre-
caution must be taken; nothing must
be allowed to seduce them from their al-

Friendship

legiance, not the most sacred ties, nor
the most solemn authority. No measure
of repression can be too stern. In that
fierce time it was natural that apostasy
should be thought worthy of death; for
apostasy from religion meant also treason
to the nation: much more those who
used their influence to seduce men to
apostasy were to be condemned. The
passage is introduced by the assertion
that if even a prophet, a recognized servant of God, attesting his prophecy with
signs and wonders, should solicit them to
leave the worship of Jehovah, in spite of
his sacred character, and in spite of the
seeming evidence of miracles, they must
turn from him with loathing, and his
doom should be death. And if the apostasy should have the weight of numbers
and a whole city go astray, the same
doom is theirs. If the tenderest relationship should tempt the soul away, if a
brother, or son, or daughter, or wife, or
friend, should entice to apostasy, the

same relentless judgment must be meted out.

The fact that this stern treatment is advocated in this Book, which is full of the most tender consideration for all weak things, shows the need of the time. Deuteronomy has some of the most beautiful legislation in favor of slaves and little children and birds and domestic animals, some of it in advance of even our modern customs and practices, permeated as these are by Christian sentiment. And it is in this finely sensitive Book that we find such strong assertion of the paramount importance of individual responsibility.

The influence of a friend or near relative is bound to be great. We are affected on every side, and at every moment, by the environment of other lives. There is a spiritual affinity, which is the closest and most powerful thing in the world, and yet in the realm of morals it has definite limits set to it. At the best

Friendship

it can only go a certain length, and ought
not to be allowed to go further than its
legitimate bounds. The writer of Deuteronomy appreciated to the full the
power and attraction of the near human
relationships. We see this from the
way he describes them, adding an ad-
ditional touch of fondness to each, "thy
brother the son of thy mother, the wife
of thy bosom, thy friend who is as
thine own soul." But it sets a limit to
the place even such tender ties should
be allowed to have. The most intimate
of relatives, the most trusted of friends,
must not be permitted to abrogate the
place of conscience. Affection may be
perverted into an instrument of evil.
There is a higher moral law than even
the law of friendship. The demands
of friendship must not be allowed to
interfere with the dictates of duty. It
is not that the moral law should be
blindly obeyed, but because in obey-
ing it we are choosing the better part

for both ; for as Frederick Robertson truly says, " the man who prefers his dearest friend to the call of duty, will soon show that he prefers himself to his dearest friend." Such weak giving in to the supposed higher demand of friendship is only a form of selfishness.

Friendship is sometimes too exacting. It asks for too much, more than we have to give, more than we ever ought to give. There is a tyranny of love, making demands which can only be granted to the loss of both. Such tyranny is a perversion of the nature of love, which is to serve, not to rule. It would override conscience, and break down the will. We cannot give up our personal duty, as we cannot give up our personal responsibility. That is how it is possible for Christ to say that if a man love father, or mother, or wife more than Him, he is not worthy of Him. No human being can take the place of God to another life ; it is an acted blasphemy to attempt it.

Friendship

There is a love which is evil in its selfishness. Its very exclusive claim is a sign of its evil root. The rights of the individual must not be renounced, even for love's sake. Human love can ask too much, and it asks too much when it would break down the individual will and conscience.

The hands that love us often are the hands
That softly close our eyes and draw us earthward.
We give them all the largesse of our life —
Not this, not all the world, contenteth them,
Till we renounce our rights as living souls.

We cannot renounce our rights as living souls without losing our souls. No man can pay the debt of life for us. No man can take the burden of life from us. To no man can we hand over the reins unreservedly. It would be cowardice, and cowardice is sin. The first axiom of the spiritual life is the sacredness of the individuality of each. We must respect each other's personality. Even when we have rights over other people, these rights

are strictly limited, and carry with them
a corresponding duty to respect their
rights also. The one intolerable despotism in the world is the attempt to
put a yoke on the souls of men, and
there are some forms of intimacy which
approach that despotism. To transgress
the moral bounds set to friendship is to
make the highest forms of friendship impossible; for these are only reached when
free spirits meet in the unity of the spirit.

The community of human life, of which
we are learning much to-day, is a great
fact. We are all bound up in the same
bundle. In a very true sense we stand
or fall together. We are ever on our
trial as a society; not only materially,
but even in the highest things, morally
and spiritually. There is a social conscience, which we affect, and which constantly affects us. We cannot rise very
much above it; to fall much below it, is
for all true purposes to cease to live. We
have recognized social standards which test

morality; we have common ties, common
duties, common responsibilities.

But with it all, in spite of the fact of
the community of human life, there is
the other fact of the singleness of human life. We have a life, which we
must live *alone*. We can never get past
the ultimate fact of the personal responsibility of each. We may be leaves from
the same tree of life, but no two leaves
are alike. We may be wrapped up in
the same bundle, but one bundle can
contain very different things. Each of
us is colored with his own shade, separate and peculiar. We have our own
special powers of intellect, our own special experience, our own moral conscience,
our own moral life to live. So, while it
is true that we stand or fall together, it
is also true — and it is a deeper truth —
that we stand or fall alone.

In this crowded world, with its intercourse and jostling, with its network of
relationships, with its mingled web of life,

we are each alone. Below the surface
there is a deep, and below the deep there
is a deeper depth. In the depth of the
human heart there is, and there must be,
solitude. There is a limit to the possible
communion with another. We never
completely open up our nature to even
our nearest and dearest. In spite of ourselves something is kept back. Not that
we are untrue in this, and hide our inner
self, but simply that we are unable to re-
veal ourselves entirely. There is a bitterness of the heart which only the heart
knoweth ; there is a joy of the heart with
which no stranger can intermeddle ; there
is a bound beyond which even a friend
who is as our own soul becomes a stranger. There is a Holy of Holies, over the
threshold of which no human feet can
pass. It is safe from trespass, guarded
from intrusion, and even we cannot give
to another the magic key to open the
door. In spite of all the complexity of
our social life, and the endless connec-

tions we form with others, there is as
the ultimate fact a great and almost weird
solitude. We may fill up our hearts with
human fellowship in all its grades, yet
there remains to each a distinct and separated life.

We speak vaguely of the mass of men,
but the mass consists of units, each with
his own life, a thing apart. The community of human life is being emphasized
to-day, and it is a lesson which bears and
needs repetition, the lesson of our common ties and common duties. But at the
same time we dare not lose sight of the
fact of the singleness of human life, if for
no other reason than that, otherwise we
have no moral appeal to make on behalf
of those ties and duties. In the region of
morals, in dealing with sin, we see how
true this solitude is. There may be what
we can truly call social and national sins,
and men can sin together, but in its ultimate issue sin is individual. It is a dis-
integrating thing, separating a man from

his fellows, and separating him from God. We are alone with our sin, like the Ancient Mariner with the bodies of his messmates around him, each cursing him with his eye. In the last issue, there is nothing in the universe but God and the single human soul. Men can share the sinning with us ; no man can share the sin. " And the sin ye do by two and two, ye must pay for one by one." Therefore in this sphere of morals there must be limits to friendship, even with the friend who is as our own soul.

Friendship is a very real and close thing. It is one of the greatest joys in life, and has noble fruits. We can do much for each other : there are burdens we can share : we can rejoice with those who do rejoice, and weep with those who weep. Through sympathy and love we are able to get out of self; and yet even here there are limits. Our helplessness in the presence of grief proves this funda-mental singleness of human life. When

Friendship

we stand beside a friend before the open
grave, under the cloud of a great sorrow,
we learn how little we can do for him.
We can only stand speechless, and pray
that the great Comforter may come with
His own divine tenderness and enter the
sanctuary of sorrow shut to feet of flesh.
Mourners have indeed been soothed by
a touch, or a look, or a prayer, which
had their source in a pitiful human heart,
but it is only as a message of condolence
flashed from one world to another. There
is a burden which every man must bear,
and none can bear for him : for there is
a personality which, even if we would, we
cannot unveil to human eyes. There are
feelings sacred to the man who feels. We
have to "dree our own weird," and live
our own life, and die our own death.

In the time of desolation, when the
truth of this solitude is borne in on us,
we are left to ourselves, not because our
friends are unfeeling, but simply because
they are unable. It is not their selfish-

ness which keeps them off, but just their frailty. Their spirit may be willing, but the flesh is weak. It is the lesson of life, that there is no stay in the arm of flesh, that even if there is no limit to human love, there is a limit to human power. Sooner or later, somewhere or other, it is the experience of every son of man, as it was the experience of the Son of Man, " Behold the hour cometh, and now is come, that ye My friends shall be scattered every man to his own, and shall leave Me alone."

Human friendship must have limits, just because it is human. It is subject to loss, and is often to some extent the sport of occasion. It lacks permanence : misunderstandings can estrange us : slander can embitter us : death can bereave us. We are left very much the victims of circumstances ; for like everything earthly it is open to change and decay. No matter how close and spiritual the intercourse, it is not permanent, and never

Friendship

certain. If nothing else, the shadow of
death is always on it. Tennyson describes how he dreamed that he and his
friend should pass through the world together, loving and trusting each other,
and together pass out into the silence.

> Arrive at last the blessed goal,
> And He that died in Holy Land
> Would reach us out the shining hand,
> And take us as a single soul.

It was a dream at the best. Neither to
live together nor to die together could
blot out the spiritual limits of friendship.
Even in the closest of human relations
when two take each other for better for
worse, for richer for poorer, in sickness
and in health, they may be made one
flesh, but never one soul. Singleness is
the ultimate fact of human life. " The
race is run by one and one, and never by
two and two."

In religion, in the deepest things of the
spirit, these limits we have been consid-

ering are perhaps felt most of all. With even a friend who is as one's own soul, we cannot seek to make a spiritual impression, without realizing the constraint of his separate individuality. We cannot break through the barriers of another's distinct existence. If we have ever sought to lead to a higher life another whom we love, we must have been made to feel that it does not all rest with us, that he is a free moral being, and that only by voluntarily yielding his heart and will and life to the King, can he enter the Kingdom. We are forced to respect his personality. We may watch and pray and speak, but we cannot save. There is almost a sort of spiritual indecency in unveiling the naked soul, in attempting to invade the personality of another life. There is sometimes a spiritual vivisection which some attempt in the name of religion, which is immoral. Only holier eyes than ours, only more reverent hands than ours, can deal with the spirit of a

Friendship

man. He is a separate individual, with
all the rights of an individual. We may
have many points of contact with him,
the contact of mind on mind, and heart
on heart ; we may even have rights over
him, the rights of love ; but he can at will
insulate his life from ours. Here also, as
elsewhere when we go deep enough into
life, it is God and the single human soul.

The lesson of all true living in every
sphere is to learn our own limitations. It
is the first lesson in art, to work within
the essential limitations of the particular
art. But in dealing with other lives it is
perhaps the hardest of all lessons, to
learn, and submit to, our limitations. It
is the crowning grace of faith, when we
are willing to submit, and to leave those
we love in the hands of God, as we leave
ourselves. Nowhere else is the limit of
friendship so deeply cut as here in the
things of the spirit.

> No man can save his brother's soul,
> Nor pay his brother's debt.

217

Friendship

Human friendship has limits because of the real greatness of man. We are too big to be quite comprehended by another. There is always something in us left unexplained, and unexplored. We do not even know ourselves, much less can another hope to probe into the recesses of our being. Friendship has a limit, because of the infinite element in the soul. It is hard to kick against the pricks, but they are meant to drive us toward the true end of living. It is hard to be brought up by a limit along any line of life, but it is designed to send us to a deeper and richer development of our life. Man's limitation is God's occasion. Only God can fully satisfy the hungry heart of man.

The Higher
Friendship

*LOVE Him, and keep Him for thy Friend, who,
   when all go away, will not forsake thee, nor
suffer thee to perish at the last.*

THOMAS À KEMPIS.

*Hush, I pray you!
What if this friend happen to be — God!*

BROWNING.

The Higher Friendship

LIFE is an education in love. There are grades and steps in it, occasions of varying opportunity for the discipline of love. It comes to us at many points, trying us at different levels, that it may get entrance somehow, and so make our lives not altogether a failure. When we give up our selfishness and isolation, even in the most rudimentary degree, a beginning is made with us that is designed to carry us far, if we but follow the leading of our hearts. There is an ideal toward which all our experience points. If it were not so, life would be a hopeless enigma, and the world a meaningless farce. There must be a spiritual function intended, a design to build up strong and true moral character, to develop sweet and holy life, otherwise

history is a despair, and experience a
hopeless riddle. All truly great human
life has been lived with a spiritual outlook, and on a high level. Men have felt
instinctively that there is no justification
for all the pain, and strife, and failure,
and sorrow of the world, if these do not
serve a higher purpose than mere existence. Even our tenderest relationships
need some more authoritative warrant
than is to be found in themselves, even in
the joy and hope they bring. That joy
cannot be meant as an empty lure to
keep life on the earth.

And spiritual man has also discovered
that the very breakdown of human ties
leads out to a larger and more permanent
love. It is sooner or later found that the
most perfect love cannot utterly satisfy
the heart of man. All our human intercourse, blessed and helpful as it may be,
must be necessarily fragmentary and
partial. A man must discover that there
is an infinite in him, which only the infi-

222

nite can match and supply. It is no dis-
paragement of human friendship to admit
this. It remains a blessed fact that it is
possible to meet devotion, which makes
us both humble and proud ; humble at
the sight of its noble sacrifice, proud with
a glad pride at its wondrous beauty.
Man is capable of the highest heights of
love. But man can never take the place
of God, and without God life is shorn of
its glory and divested of its meaning.

So the human heart has ever craved for
a relationship, deeper and more lasting
than any possible among men, undis-
turbed by change, unmenaced by death,
unbroken by fear, unclouded by doubt.
The limitations and losses of earthly
friendship are meant to drive us to the
higher friendship. Life is an education
in love, but the education is not complete till we learn the love of the eternal.
Ordinary friendship has done its work
when the limits of friendship are reached,
when through the discipline of love we

are led into a larger love, when a door is opened out to a higher life. The sickness of heart which is the lot of all, the loneliness which not even the voice of a friend can dispel, the grief which seems to stop the pulse of life itself, find their final meaning in this compulsion toward the divine. We are sometimes driven out not knowing whither we go, not knowing the purpose of it; only knowing through sheer necessity that here we have no abiding city, or home, or life, or love; and seeking a city, a home, a life, a love, that hath foundations.

We have some training in the love of friends, as if only to prove to us that without love we cannot live. All our intimacies are but broken lights of the love of God. They are methods of preparation for the great communion. In so far even that our earthly friendships are helps to life, it is because they are shot through with the spiritual, and they prepare us by their very deficiencies for

something more permanent. There have
been implanted in man an instinct, and a
need, which make him discontented, till
he find content in God. If at any time
we are forced to cease from man, whose
breath is in his nostrils, it is that we may
reach out to the infinite Father, unchang-
ing, the same yesterday, to-day, and forever. This is the clamant, imperious need
of man.

The solitude of life in its ultimate issue
is because we were made for a higher
companionship. It is just in the inner-
most sanctuary, shut to every other visit-
ant, that God meets us. We are driven
to God by the needs of the heart. If the
existence of God was due to a purely intellectual necessity; if we believed in Him
only because our reason gave warrant for
the faith; it would not matter much
whether He really is, and whether we
really can know Him. But when the
instincts of our nature, and the necessities of the heart-life demand God, we

15   225

are forced to believe. In moments of deep feeling, when all pretence is silenced, a man may be still able to question the *existence* of God, but he does not question his own *need* of God. Man, to remain man, must believe in the possibility of this relationship with the divine. There is a love which passeth the love of women, passeth the love of comrades, passeth all earthly love, the love of God to the weary, starved heart of man.

To believe in this great fact does not detract from human friendship, but really gives it worth and glory. It is because of this, that all love has a place in the life of man. All our worships, and friendships, and loves, come from God, and are but reflections of the divine tenderness. All that is beautiful, and lovely and pure, and of good repute, finds its appropriate setting in God; for it was made by God. He made it for Himself. He made man with instincts, and aspirations, and heart-hunger, and divine unrest, that He might give them full satisfaction in Himself. He claims everything, but He gives everything. Our human relationships are sanctified and glorified by the spiritual union. He gives us back our kinships, and friendships, with a new light on them, an added tenderness, transfiguring our common ties and intimacies, flooding them with a supernal joy. We part from men to meet with God, that we may be able to meet men again on a higher platform. But the love of God is the end and design of all other loves. If the flowers and leaves fade, it is that the time of ripe fruit is at hand. If these adornments are taken from the tree of life, it is to make room for the supreme fruitage. Without the love of God all other love would be but deception, luring men on to the awful disillusionment. We were born for the love of God; if we do not find it, it were better for us if we had never been born. We may have tasted of all the joys the

The Higher

world can offer, have known success and
the gains of success, been blessed with
the sweetest friendships and the fiercest
loves; but if we have not found this the
chief end of life, we have missed our
chance, and can only have at the last a
desolated life.

But if through the joy or through the
sorrow of life, through love or the want
of it, through the gaining of friends or
the loss of them, we have been led to
dower our lives with the friendship of
God, we are possessed of the incorrup-
tible, and undefiled, and that passeth not
away. The man who has it has attained
the secret cheaply, though it had to be
purchased with his heart's blood, with
the loss of his dream of blessedness.
When the fabric of life crumbled to its
native dust, and he rose out of its wreck,
the vision of the eternal love came with
the thrill of a great revelation. It was the
entrance into the mystery, and the wonder of it awed him, and the joy of it

inspired him, and he awakened to the fact that never again could he be *alone* to all eternity.

Communion with God is the great fact of life. All our forms of worship, all our ceremonies and symbols of religion, find their meaning here. There is, it is true, an ethic of religion, certain moral teachings valuable for life : there are truths of religion to be laid hold of by the reason : there are the consolations of religion to comfort the heart : but the root of all religion is this mystical union, a communion with the Unseen, a friendship with God open to man. Religion is not an acceptance of a creed, or a burden of commandments, but a personal secret of the soul, to be attained each man for himself. It is the experience of the nearness of God, the mysterious contact with the divine, and the consciousness that we stand in a special individual relationship with Him. The first state of exaltation, when the knowledge burst upon the soul, cannot, of course, last; but its effect remains in inward peace, and outward impulse toward nobler life.

Men of all ages have known this close relationship. The possibility of it is the glory of life: the fact of it is the romance of history, and the true reading of history. All devout men that have ever lived have lived in the light of this communion. All religious experience has had this in common, that somehow the soul is so possessed by God, that doubt of His existence ceases; and the task of life becomes to keep step with Him, so that there may be correspondence between the outer and the inner conditions of life. Men have known this communion in such a degree that they have been called preeminently the Friends of God, but something of the experience which underlies the term is true of the pious of all generations.

To us, in our place in history, communion with God comes through Jesus

230

Friendship

Christ. It is an ineffable mystery, but it is still a fact of experience. Only through Jesus do we know God, His interest in us, His desire for us, His purpose with us. He not only shows us in His own example the blessedness of a life in fellowship with the Father, but He makes it possible for us. United to Jesus, we know ourselves united to God. The power of Jesus is not limited to the historical impression made by His life. It entered the world as history; it lives in the world as spiritual fact to-day. Luther's experience is the experience of all believers, "To me it is not simply an old story of an event that happened once; for it is a gift, a bestowing, that endures forever." We offer Christ the submission of our hearts, and the obedience of our lives; and He offers us His abiding presence. We take Him as our Master; and He takes us as His friends. "I call you no longer servants," He said to His disciples, "but I have called you friends."

The Higher

The servant knoweth not what his Mas
ter doeth, his only duty is to obey; a
friend is admitted to confidence, and
though he may do the same thing as a
servant, he does not do it any longer un-
reasoningly, but, having been taken into
counsel, he knows why he is doing it.
This was Christ's method with His disciples, not to apportion to each his task,
but to show them His great purpose for
the world, and to ask for their service
and devotion to carry it out.

The distinction is not that a servant
pleases his master, and a friend pleases
himself. It is that our Lord takes us up
into a relationship of love with Himself,
and we go out into life inspired with His
spirit to work His work. It begins with
the self-surrender of love; and love, not
fear nor favor, becomes the motive. To
feel thus the touch of God on our lives
changes the world. Its fruits are joy,
and peace, and confidence that all the
events of life are suffused, not only with

Friendship

meaning, but with a meaning of love.
The higher friendship brings a satisfaction of the heart, and a joy commensu-
rate to the love. Its reward is itself, the
sweet, enthralling relationship, not any
adventitious gain it promises, either in
the present, or for the future. Even if
there were no physical, or moral, rewards
and punishments in the world, we would
still love and serve Christ *for His own
sake.* The soul that is bound by this
personal attachment to Jesus has a life in
the eternal, which transfigures the life in
time with a great joy.

We can see at once that to be the
friend of God will mean peace also. It
has brought peace over the troubled lives
of all His friends throughout the ages.
Every man who enters into the covenant,
knows the world to be a spiritual arena,
in which the love of God manifests itself.
He walks no longer on a sodden earth
and under a gray sky; for he knows that,
though all men misunderstand him, he

is understood, and followed with loving sympathy, in heaven. It was this confidence in God as a real and near friend, which gave to Abraham's life such distinction, and the calm repose which made his character so impressive. Strong in the sense of God's friendship, he lived above the world, prodigal of present possessions, because sure of the future, waiting securely in the hope of the great salvation. He walked with God in sweet unaffected piety, and serene faith, letting his character ripen in the sunshine, and living out his life as unto God not unto men. To know the love of God does not mean the impoverishing of our lives, by robbing them of their other sweet relations. Rather, it means the enriching of these, by revealing their true beauty and purpose. Sometimes we are brought nearer God through our friends, if not through their influence or the joy of their love, then through the discipline which comes from their very limitations

Friendship

and from their loss. But oftener the experience has been that, through our union with the Friend of friends, we are led into richer and fuller intercourse with our fellows. The nearer we get to the centre of the circle, the nearer we get to each other. To be joined together in Christ is the only permanent union, deeper than the tie of blood, higher than the bond of kin, closer than the most sacred earthly relationship. Spiritual kinship is the great nexus to unite men. "Who are My brethren?" asked Jesus, and for answer pointed to His disciples, and added, "Whosoever shall do the will of My Father in heaven the same is My mother and sister and brother."

We ought to make more of our Christian friendships, the communion of the saints, the fellowship of believers. "They that feared God spake often one with another," said the prophet Malachi in one of the darkest hours of the church. What mutual comfort, and renewed hope,

The Higher

they would get from, and give to, each other! Faith can be increased, and love stimulated, and enthusiasm revived by intercourse. The supreme friendship with Christ therefore will not take from us any of our treasured intimacies, unless they are evil. It will increase the number of them, and the true force of them. It will link us on to all who love the same Lord in sincerity and truth. It will open our heart to the world of men that Jesus loved and gave His life to save.

This friendship with the Lord knows no fear of loss; neither life, nor death, nor things present, nor things to come can separate us. It is joy and strength in the present, and it lights up the future with a great hope. We are not much concerned about speculations regarding the future; for we know that we are in the hands of our Lover. All that we care to assert of the future is, that Christ will in an ever fuller degree be the environment of all Christian souls, and the effect of that constant environment will fulfil the aspiration of the apostle, "We shall be like Him, for we shall see Him as He is." Communion produces likeness. This even now is the test of our friendship with the Lord. Are we assimilating His mind, His way of looking at things, His judgments, His spirit? Is the Christ-conscience being developed in us? Have we an increasing interest in the things which interest Him, an increasing love of the things that He loves, an increasing desire to serve the purposes He has at heart? "Ye are My friends if ye do whatsoever I command you," is the test by which we can try ourselves.

Fellowship with Him, being much in His company, thinking of Him, seeking to please Him, will produce likeness, and bring us together on more intimate terms. For, as love leads to the desire for fuller fellowship ; so fellowship leads to a deeper love. Even if sometimes we almost doubt whether we are really in this blessed covenant of friendship, our policy is to go on loving Him, serving Him, striving to please Him; and we will yet receive the assurance, which will bring peace; He will not disappoint us at the last. It is worth all the care and effort we can give, to have and to keep Him for our friend who will be a lasting possession, whose life enters into the very fibre of our life, and whose love makes us certain of God.

We ought to use our faith in this friendship to bless our lives. To have an earthly friend, whom we trust and reverence, can be to us a source of strength, keeping us from evil, making us ashamed of evil. The dearer the friend and the more spiritual the friendship, the keener will be this feeling, and the more needful does it seem to keep the garments clean. It must reach its height of intensity and of moral effectiveness in the case of friendship with God. There can be no motive on earth

so powerful. If we could only have such
a friendship, we see at once what an influence it might have over our life. We
can appreciate more than the joy, and
peace, and comfort of it; we can feel the
power of it. To know ourselves ever before a living, loving Presence, having a
constant sense of Christ abiding in us,
taking Him with us into the market-
place, into our business and our pleasure,
to have Him as our familiar friend in joy
and sorrow, in gain and loss, in success
and failure, must, in accordance with all
psychological law, be a source of strength,
lifting life to a higher level of thought, and
feeling, and action. Supposing it were
true and possible, it would naturally be
the strongest force in the world, the most
effective motive that could be devised: it
would affect the whole moral outlook,
and make some things easy now deemed
impossible, and make some things impossible now to our shame too easy.
Supposing this covenant with God were

true, and we knew ourselves to have such a Lover of our soul, it would, as a matter of course, give us deeper and more serious views of human life, and yet take away from us the burden and the unrest of life.

Unless history be a lie, and experience a delusion, it *is* true. The world is vocal with a chorus of witness to the truth of it. From all sorts and conditions of men comes the testimony to its reality — from the old, who look forward to this Friend to make their bed in dying; from the young, who know His aid in the fiery furnace of temptation; from the strong, in the burden of the day and the dust of the battle, who know the rest of His love even in the sore labor; from the weak, who are mastered by His gracious pity, and inspired by His power to suffer and to bear. Christ's work on earth was to make the friendship of God possible to all. It seems too good to be true, too wondrous a condescension on His part, but its reality has been tested, and at-

Friendship

tested, by generations of believers. This covenant of friendship is open to us, to be ours in life, and in death, and past the gates of death.

The human means of communication is prayer, though we limit it sadly. Prayer is not an act of worship merely, the bending of the knee on set occasions, and offering petitions in need. It is an attitude of soul, opening the life on the Godward side, and keeping free communication with the world of spirit. And so, it is possible to pray always, and to keep our friendship ever green and sweet : and God comes back upon the life, as dew upon the thirsty ground. There is an interchange of feeling, a responsiveness of love, a thrill of mutual friendship.

> You must love Him, ere to you '
> He shall seem worthy of your love.

The great appeal of the Christian faith is to Christian experience. Loving Christ

is its own justification, as every loving
heart knows. Life evidences itself: the
existence of light is its own proof. The
power of Christ on the heart needs no
other argument than itself. Men only
doubt when the life has died out, and
the light has waned, and flickered, and
spent itself. It is when there is no sign
of the spirit in our midst, no token of
forces beyond the normal and the usual,
that we can deny the spirit. It is when
faith is not in evidence that we can dispute faith. It is when love is dead that
we can question love. The Christian
faith is not a creed, but a life; not a
proposition, but a passion. Love is its
own witness to the soul that loves: communion is its own attestation to the spirit
that lives in the fellowship. The man
who lives with Jesus knows Him to be a
Lover that cleaves closer than a brother,
a Friend that loveth at all times, and a
Brother born for adversity.

It does not follow that there is an end

of the question, so far as we are concerned, if we say that we at least do not
know that friendship, and cannot love
Him. Some even say it with a wistful
longing, " Oh, that I knew where I might
find Him." It is true that love cannot be
forced, that it cannot be made to order,
that we cannot love because we ought,
or even because we want. But we can
bring ourselves into the presence of the
lovable. We can enter into Friendship
through the door of Discipleship; we
can learn love through service; and the
day will come to us also when the Master's word will be true, " I call you no
longer servant, but I call you friend."
His love will take possession of us, till all
else seems as hatred in comparison. " All
lovers blush when ye stand beside Christ,"
says Samuel Rutherford; " woe unto all
love but the love of Christ. Shame forevermore be upon all glory but the glory
of Christ; hunger forevermore be upon
all heaven but Christ. I cry death, death

Friendship

be upon all manner of life but the life of Christ."

To be called *friends* by our Master, to know Him as the Lover of our souls, to give Him entrance to our hearts, is to learn the meaning of living, and to experience the ecstasy of living. The Higher Friendship is bestowed without money and without price, and is open to every heart responsive to God's great love.

> 'T is only heaven that is given away,
> 'T is God alone may be had for the asking.